Considering Hate

CONSIDERING HATE

Violence, Goodness, and Justice in
American Culture and Politics

KAY WHITLOCK and
MICHAEL BRONSKI

Beacon Press
Boston

BEACON PRESS
Boston, Massachusetts
www.beacon.org

Beacon Press books
are published under the auspices of
the Unitarian Universalist Association of Congregations.

18 17 16 15   8 7 6 5 4 3 2 1

This book is printed on acid-free paper that meets the uncoated paper
ANSI/NISO specifications for permanence as revised in 1992.

Text design and composition by Kim Arney

Library of Congress Cataloging-in-Publication Data
Whitlock, Kay.
    Considering hate : violence, goodness, and justice in American culture and politics /
Kay Whitlock, Michael Bronski.
        pages   cm
    Includes bibliographical references and index.
    ISBN 978-0-8070-9191-3 (hardback)
    ISBN 978-0-8070-9192-0 (ebook)
    1. Hate—United States. 2. Violence—United States. 3. Discrimination—United
States. 4. Multiculturalism—United States. 5. United States—Race relations.
I. Bronski, Michael. II. Title.
    HN90.M84W45 2014
    303.60973—dc23
                                                    2014017917

CONTENTS

AUTHORS' NOTE

Violence directed against vulnerable communities has been a focus of our work as activists and writers for many years. We've been thinking about the ways that belief in the superiority of some groups and the inferiority of others is foundational to American society; we've been reflecting on what this has to do with how justice is understood and administered in America.

This book emerges from our individual and joint histories. Our inquiry is political, philosophical, psychological, and theological. Significantly, because both of us have always been fascinated by popular culture and its history, our inquiry is also cultural.

KAY WHITLOCK

I am a progressive activist and independent scholar closing in on five decades of organizing and writing about a broad range of social and economic justice topics. Despite growing up in a politically conservative, working-class family in southern Colorado, by the late 1960s I was immersed in the anti–Vietnam War movement and support work for farmworkers' organizing struggles. These were not abstract commitments but responses to my own observations and experiences and the result of listening deeply to others who challenged me to "think differently." By the 1970s, I was deeply involved in anti-racism work, feminism, environmental struggles, and an emergent lesbian and gay rights movement (although I felt much more at home when I just started calling myself "queer.") All of these commitments intersect and reflect essential parts of myself; they're never about "those people who need help." That I am a Buddhist practitioner also influences how I think about and experience the world.

I've always existed at the borders of mainstream engagement and radical perspective, a location that is in equal parts a blessing and a curse for all sorts of complicated reasons. But I'm there, in part, because from early on I learned the importance of not writing off people just because they don't share my opinions. My experience taught me that the building of relationship and community isn't simply about hunkering down with people who are just like me. My love/hate relationship with popular culture, apparently present from birth, gave me a profound passion for learning from the wildly divergent stories that people—and societies—tell about themselves and one another.

I am most publicly identified with work related to a critique of hate crime laws, the broader conceptual hate frame that so significantly shapes public understanding of violence and justice, and the criminalization of LGBT people in the United States. All of my work has sought to help expose structural forms of violence.

To me, these are intricate areas of inquiry that plunge straight into the heart of how one understands the meaning of community and relationship. In a sense, they constitute a form of social justice teaching riddle: Who am I without a hated and inferior enemy to hold up the mirror so that I may see my own face?

In 2001, just months before the tragic violence of 9/11, the American Friends Service Committee (AFSC) published *In a Time of Broken Bones: A Call to Dialogue on Hate Violence and the Limitations of Hate*

Crime Legislation. This working paper, which I authored, presented AFSC's understanding of the symbiotic relationship between hate violence and structural violence and was circulated widely within social justice circles. Because it questioned the assumptions on which hate crime laws were based, it was immediately controversial.

AFSC was not the only progressive voice raising specific concerns about hate crime laws. Around the same time, so did Carolina Cordero Dyer, then a board member of New York City's Audre Lorde Project, a center for community organizing among lesbian, gay, bisexual, Two Spirit, transgender, and gender-nonconforming people of color. Yasmin Nair, a Chicago-based activist and academic, was underscoring some of the problems inherent in hate crime laws. And an increasing number of organizations also began speaking out, most of them led by and primarily serving women, transgender, and queer communities of color.

Most striking to me is how many liberal and progressive people and organizations responded to these respectful dissents from hate crime orthodoxy with anger or attempts to silence or marginalize them. This tension is symptomatic of a larger societal unwillingness to come to terms with structural forms of violence—especially, but not only, racism. It's a refusal that, to the detriment of all, runs like an artery through American culture and politics.

What would happen if we did have that larger conversation about the hate frame? Could any good come of it? *Considering Hate* says yes.

MICHAEL BRONSKI

I have been involved in gay liberation since 1969. Before that I was active in civil rights work and in the anti–Vietnam War movement. For most of my life I have been engaged as a writer, journalist, independent scholar, activist, and organizer. Beginning in the 1970s I worked closely with the LGBT press and publishing worlds. In the 1980s I was involved with AIDS activism. During that time I published extensively in the lesbian and gay press, as well as the mainstream press, on issues of sexuality, culture, politics, and sex. In 2000 I was asked to teach a course on LGBT studies at Dartmouth and took my grassroots experience into the academy. This change of career continued when I became Professor of the Practice in Activism and Media in the Studies of Women, Gender, and Sexuality at Harvard University.

Although the trip from *Fag Rag*—the first national gay male periodical in the country, on which I worked in the 1970s—to Harvard has been curious, the one constant has been my desire to examine and explore interactions between culture and politics, between people's lived lives and how we discuss them intellectually. From an early age, as a self-identified gay boy, I understood the world was not as welcoming or as good as it could or should be. This understanding fueled my political involvements as well as my writing, whether in theater criticism, political commentary, or social history. It was an experience and lesson deeply ingrained. Writing *Considering Hate* is a continuation of that.

INTRODUCTION

"Terrible is the temptation to do good."
—BERTOLT BRECHT, *The Caucasian Chalk Circle*

In considering how central hate is to American discussions about violence and injustice, we wondered why the equally important concepts of goodness and justice were almost always missing. As we began to write about this absence, we realized we needed definitions of these terms that would illuminate and guide our ideas.

Goodness: An awareness, translated into action, of the intrinsic worth and interdependence of all peoples and ecologies, and the determination to dismantle societal structures that support social inequalities and the violence that accompanies them.

Justice: The evolving pursuit of trustworthy, respectful, and non-exploitative relationships, together with accountability for interrupting, preventing, and redressing violence, in its myriad forms, against individuals, peoples, communities, and ecologies.

■　■　■

Hate haunts the human imagination. It is a primal response that engages an individual with the world. By establishing clear personal,

1

social, and political boundaries, it allows us to situate ourselves as people and groups in larger, complex contexts. We feel hate, even revel in it, because it helps us separate good from evil—and therefore helps us survive. Because it is so emotionally charged, hate often makes us feel alive. We experience it as an anchor for safety, because it readily slots segments of the population into "us" and "them." We know where we stand: with the good people who are hated by the bad people, or the good people who hate the bad people. Yet the safety we feel is inextricably bound to the anxiety that hate also generates. We know it can engender a counter-hate from the people and groups we despise, thus placing us, arguably, in more danger than before. Tellingly, most people experience themselves not as haters, but as the hated. When they do express hate, it is inevitably in response to *being* hated. People are hesitant to claim the prerogative to hate without cause. However, once they feel that someone, or some group, hates them, they have no problem accessing their own hate.

Hate is a language (not to be confused with "hate speech," a political and legal concept) that orders the world. People commonly think of hate as an out-of-control, even obliterating emotion—someone is "consumed by hate" or "eaten up by hate"—as if its existence eradicates the person experiencing it. This can be an intense personal experience. From time to time, many people resort to the language of hate—"I hate you!"—to express the virulent anger felt toward individuals who have caused personal hurt. "I hate that" registers profound individual dislike of something as trivial as a particular food. Hate is also a political and social concept that allows individuals and groups to negotiate a world that feels unsafe. *Considering Hate* is about the ways in which the intense animus described as hatred is politically mobilized, and how hate as a political frame shapes societal views about violence and effective responses to it.

Do all humans hate? If hate is employed to navigate danger, is it hardwired in human identity? The answer is unknowable. We cannot extract human emotions from the cultural contexts in which they are named. What interests us here is how the concept of hate has evolved and how it functions today. The question is not so much why individuals and entire communities may have this feeling, but how they use it and how it constructs, through language and symbols, the material world and human actions in it.

One of the most noted "hate crimes" in recent US history was the 1998 murder of Matthew Shepard. On October 7, 1998, Shepard, an openly gay, twenty-one-year-old, middle-class, white University of Wyoming student, was robbed and beaten to death by Aaron McKinney and Russell Henderson, two methamphetamine-addicted, economically disadvantaged men his own age. The murder was immediately characterized as a hate crime even though Wyoming's penal code had no such classification. There was no evidence that Shepard was murdered because he was gay, although this may have played a part in his being selected as a robbery victim. Labeling it a "hate crime," the media highlighted issues of anti-gay violence. At the same time this classification obscured the issues of class, poverty, and gender that also defined the murder.[1]

Many in the United States are wedded to using hate to explain our personal interactions and political ideologies. Society has created a "hate frame" in order to explain violence, seek justice, and attempt to understand human goodness. What would it look like to disentangle hate from justice and replace the language of hate with that of goodness?

Compare the Matthew Shepard case to the noted 2012 rape that took place in Steubenville, Ohio. On August 12, 2012, Trent Mays and Ma'lik Richmond, two high school football players, were accused and, months later, convicted of sexually assaulting a highly intoxicated sixteen-year-old female student from a neighboring high school at a large, out-of-control party. Fellow students witnessed the assault, disseminated photos on social media, and openly discussed it. The media coverage was filled with outrage, but the words *hate* and *hate crime* were never used. News reporting and commentary highlighted issues of teenage drinking, male sports culture, and the desensitizing impact of social media. There was some media discussion of the prevalence of rape and sexual violence in the United States, but almost no attempt was made to contextualize the assault as an example of the socially accepted hatred or animus toward women.

The language of hate, or its absence, shapes how so many individuals and institutions understand and order the world. It prioritizes events, actions, people, groups, and beliefs. It helps define the self in relationship to righteousness, fairness, and justice. Society labels certain illegal acts as hate crimes because, morally and legally, it has been decided that they were motivated by a clear animus against a specific person or group because of their religion, race, sexual orientation, gender, gender expression, disability, or ethnicity. Members of the media ask, Why did the 9/11 hijackers hate America? News stories describe anti-gay slurs in high school hallways as "hate speech." Yet society does not generally define violence against women as motivated by hate. Nor do most people think of New York's stop-and-frisk policing policy—overwhelmingly aimed at young men of color—as motivated by hate. We want to examine what individuals and groups mean when they use the word *hate*. What are the personal, social, and cultural impacts and consequences of the language of hate? How does hate work?

Considering Hate is not, in the end, about hate at all. Hate is an easy placeholder for a complex web of many other concepts. These concepts are integral to ideas of personhood, justice, fairness, and goodness. On a larger scale, they are foundational to our understanding of society and culture. The "hate frame" provides a clear, quickly grasped, emotionally and psychically comfortable context in which to consider our inchoate, and frequently unexamined, ideas of what it means to be human, reflect goodness in our lives, and seek justice.

Considering Hate does not argue that people and groups cannot possess an animus influenced by prejudice against and ignorance of others that can result in physically and emotionally damaging actions; history and contemporary life demonstrate that they can. What we are arguing is that the reflexive labeling of these emotions and actions as hate obscures the multiplicity of factors that help explain them. It also prevents people from understanding the complex ways in which they are structured.

Violence, in particular large-scale public violence, elicits a tangle of confusing emotions and ideas linked to multilayered histories and contexts. The quickest, most readily grasped way to make sense of this is to rely on the hate frame. The bombings at the Boston Marathon on April 15, 2013, in which three died and 264 were injured, is a good example. Almost immediately, though no suspects or motives were evident, comparisons were drawn to 9/11—rather than to the April 19, 1995, Oklahoma City bombing by American citizens to protest the actions of the federal government—and commentators concluded that the perpetrators "hated America." When the suspects were identified as Tamerlan and Dzhokhar Tsarnaev, Chechen brothers rumored to hold extremist Islamic political beliefs, these assertions seemed to be confirmed. The unexpectedness of the bombing, the great number of injuries, and the lack of apparent motivation allowed the mainstream news media to reflexively use the hate frame (hate was described as "terror") as a way to avoid a more sophisticated inquiry.

Such a response was predictable. The hate frame often provides the only language we have to explain such an event. The reflexive use of hate as an explanation always reinforces its use, even if the facts do not fit the explanation. The hate frame is culturally determined. It encompasses the political spectrum and implicates us all.

As more facts emerged about the Boston bombing, including that both Tsarnaevs were assimilated Americans and that Dzhokhar was a popular, even beloved, athlete in high school and college, it made little sense: the brothers did not fit the preconceptions. As Chechen Muslims they defied the commonplace assumption that all Muslims are Arabs. And prior to the bombing, the FBI had approached Tamerlan Tsarnaev, requesting that he serve as an informant, providing them with reporting on the Chechen and Muslim communities.

The hate frame prevents examination of many types of violence embedded in American culture, some accepted or taken for granted, some not. It also prevents us from examining whom violence is directed against and why. Often violence is seen as spontaneous, such as intimate partner violence; sometimes as "legitimate," such as police violence. In reality, such violence is structural—that is, embedded in cultural norms—and is frequently unseen and unchallenged. These forms of violence are almost never labeled as expressions of hate. The selective use of the language of hate—in some cases reflecting a rush to judgment, and in others, virtually never applied—obscures and purposefully ignores social and cultural power relationships that may help us understand the causes of multiple forms of violence. Only by understanding the actual causes of violence—is it used to oppress a person or group? to resist oppression? to assert independence? to assert control?—can we begin to comprehend what fairness or justice might mean in these situations.

The larger question is, why do concepts such as justice, fairness, and goodness coalesce around hate? Why has hate, and its attendant violence and reliance on retribution, become so central to American culture? Why is it so important? Why are so many people fascinated, even obsessed with it? Daily news headlines warn that the slightest change in Middle Eastern politics may produce international terrorists. Since 1988 multiple versions of television's hugely popular *Law and Order* series, which thrive in reruns, impress on audiences the endless dangers of American life and the need to convict and imprison perpetrators. In the summer of 2013, during the Trayvon Martin murder trial, the nation was transfixed with the question of whether George Zimmerman committed a hate crime.

"Hate" infiltrates our language in the most casual ways. LGBT activists refer to homophobic politicians and religious people as "haters." The phrase "haters gonna hate" is ubiquitous, employed by both the Right and the Left to characterize opponents. Using military metaphors and conjuring incipient violence, conservatives blithely assert that liberals have declared a "war on Christmas." Liberals, just as blithely, claim that conservatives have declared a "war on women."

The hate frame reinscribes cultural, political, and emotional structures that cause and reinforce cycles of hate. This is evident in the escalation of the United States' "war on terror" against those who "hate American freedom." Vehement debate pervades the media over the increased use of waterboarding and other forms of "enhanced interrogation," targeted political assassination, and the use of drones for foreign and domestic spying. Groups considered by the United States to be terrorist in turn accuse the United States of terrorism. Often, allied and non-allied countries accuse the United States of using methods they consider to be terrorist, provoking a like response.

These cyclical events are not new; they exist, for elusive reasons, throughout history. Do humans simply have difficulty changing entrenched cultural and political habits? Do we value an illusory feeling of safety over the fear of an unknown future? Are humans, as Sigmund Freud postulated in *Civilization and Its Discontents* with his theory of the "death drive," bent on self-destruction because of internal conflicts between personal freedom and necessary repression?

The foundational question here is not so much "how can we change this?" as "do we, as humans, want to move beyond cultural expectations that replicate and reinforce destructive behavior?" *Considering Hate* raises questions that often go unasked, or when asked are met with hostility and dismissal. All too often they are never even imagined.

We are not claiming, simplistically, that the United States is filled with hatred, but rather that there are structural elements in the culture that are integral to promoting and reinforcing social power imbalances. These imbalances lead to individual and group violence. This violence is often understood to emanate from individual choices, cultural differences, or personal prejudice. *Considering Hate* makes the case that these individual and personal emotions, ideas, and acts are intimately connected to larger institutionalized structures of power and inequality.

We are not suggesting that some individuals don't feel and exhibit animus centered on race, gender, ethnic, sexual, or other differences. Such people exist, and they do harm to other people and groups. We argue, rather, that individuals act violently, and are encouraged to act this way, because of larger social and culture influences that society doesn't always consciously comprehend. Italian political philosopher Antonio Gramsci referred to the existence of larger cultural forces that shape individual choices as "hegemony." These influences, controlling narratives, touch every person's life. Individuals are responsible for their beliefs and actions—to deny this would deny the integrity of personhood—but it would be naive to think human beings are not also influenced by their surroundings.

Considering Hate does not argue that society simply needs policies that are more fair and just. Fair and just laws are critical, yet structural violence and injustice are not dismantled simply through laws and political reform. If these efforts are to be lasting and effective, they must also be rooted in cultural strategies that radically influence our imaginations, that set us free to envision alternatives beyond the choices offered us by those in power, that encourage and strengthen ideas of goodness sufficient to bolster structural change.

We do not hold that everything would be better if only people loved one another. Rather, we call for deeper thinking about how all of us use terms such as *violence, fairness, justice, innocence, guilt, responsibility,* and *goodness.*

How, over the course of US history and culture, did the idea of hate gain precedence as a factor organizing our social and legal imagination? By tracking the evolution of the hate frame, we hope to understand the power it has today. Comprehending this will allow us as a nation to grapple with the problems that now face us.

We believe that change, even if incomplete, is possible. More important, we believe that change is a process comprising thinking, learning, and acting. We will examine the cultural and social structures that lead to the unending cycle of producing more hate and less goodness and almost never any justice. We call for a paradigm shift in how we as a nation, and as individuals, think about hate.

We suggest something both audaciously simple and incredibly ambitious: the redefining of basic concepts of justice and goodness. For the most part, the words *justice* and *goodness* are superficially meaningful, but vague and amorphous. They have political, even spiritual, meaning but are used sentimentally, without moral depth. This inexactness of concrete meaning is partially a result of an impoverished use of language. Just as traditional definitions of hate engender feelings of security, traditional assumptions about justice evoke good feeling without the demand for action or change. What would it mean to seek justice in the largest, most profound sense of the word? What would it mean to act with goodness, a far more elusive concept than justice?

Because definitions of hate, justice, and goodness are open-ended, expansive, and interpreted differently, readers will encounter developing definitions of these terms throughout this book. We will draw on the thinking and writing of individuals including the Reverend Martin Luther King Jr., Simone Weil, Angela Y. Davis, Eduardo Bonilla-Silva, James H. Cone, Hannah Arendt, Edward Said, Jean-Paul Sartre, Lillian Smith, Audre Lorde, James Baldwin, Toni Morrison, Walter Brueggemann, Slavoj Zizek, and Lewis Hyde.

Society thinks of concepts such as hate, fairness, or goodness as personal attributes: a person hates, a judge rules fairly or unfairly, someone does good. *Considering Hate* moves this discussion from the realm of the personal to the public. It is concerned with the connection between the personal and the public and how the concept of civic goodness can be politically transformative.

This political and moral transformation from the personal to the public, the individual to the civic, is imperative for creating lasting social change. *Considering Hate* seeks to promote discussions that encourage readers to imagine a society radically different from the one we have now. It does not recommend specific changes in public policy. Changes that grow out of a substantial restructuring of social and economic relationships should not replicate existing power dynamics.

We hope readers will begin to think differently and carry these new visions into their lives and work. *Considering Hate* seeks to shift the focus of public policy from a preoccupation with the enemy to questions of how to dismantle the structures that lead to and institutionalize violence. What alternative approaches hold greater promise for reducing entrenched patterns of dehumanization and violence?

Political change happens in numerous ways. But it always begins with the imagination. New realities must be imagined before they are constructed. Imagination is not wishful thinking. It is the first practical step toward articulating new possibilities.

None of this is easy. The narrator in Bertolt Brecht's *Caucasian Chalk Circle* notes that "terrible is the temptation to do good." Brecht's ironic aphorism exposes the heart of the human dilemma. Many people want to do good—act ethically, act morally, help people—but that impulse is often fraught with problems, made difficult by social and political circumstance. Often enacting goodness is seen not as an opportunity but a temptation to be avoided. We hope to challenge that idea.

This shift to a more clearly articulated framework and language of goodness can only begin if we understand how deeply ingrained hate is in society, and how powerfully, in mythic ways, it is kept alive in the public imagination. Four salient myths about hate profoundly shape society:

1. *Hate is rooted in irrational personal prejudice, fear and loathing of difference, lack of tolerance and appreciation for others who "aren't like me," and ignorance of other races/cultures/religions.*

   The individual experience of hating someone or some group is a powerful one. As humans we can be consumed by hate, and this intense emotion can make us commit acts that appear as "irrational" as they are horrific. Personal prejudice is never entirely *personal*—it is always supported by social and political ideologies that shape and reinforce it. Examining these structures, and not always focusing on the individual, will give us a far better understanding of how hate works.

2. *"Hate is hate." The historical and contemporary specificities of violence directed against communities of color, queers, immigrants, women, Muslims, Jews, and others do not matter. Hate is about prejudice. It is not about power relationships or institutional policies in any foundational way.*

There is a deep cultural impulse to condemn hate wholesale, to totalize it as a single emotion. People do this because hate is a powerful, frightening emotion and we are often overwhelmed when thinking about it. But the emotion and the enactment of hate have histories that overlap and diverge from one another. Animus aimed at one group has specific historical and cultural roots based on the experiences of the hated and the haters. To ignore these is to ignore the roots of hate, and, just as important, how hate actually affects people.

3. *Hate violence is perpetrated by individual extremists, loners, and misfits who violate basic, commonly agreed upon standards of fairness.*

The media love stories of lone gunmen, disgruntled loners, the crazy student who opens fire in the hallways of a school. These are seductive narratives that stir our imaginations but obscure reality. Individuals do act on their own will, and the world is full of people who, for numerous reasons, commit terrible acts. But this all takes place in a context. There are no isolated incidents of violence and no isolated killers. Finding the balance between individual will and social pressure can be complicated, but to avoid this is to misunderstand and misrepresent hate.

4. *Hate violence is unacceptable to respectable society.*

Americans believe that hate violence is completely anathema to respectable society. This deeply held belief is difficult to shake, in part because when violence does occur, some person or group sees and speaks against it—that is how it is noticed and reported. But the majority of Americans want to believe that respectable society—a category whose very construction excludes those deemed unrespectable—does not tolerate violence. Yet throughout American history, animus-based violence against individuals and groups has been accepted, even celebrated. Popularly supported wars against Native peoples and the widespread lynching of African Americans are two clear examples.

■　■　■

Two distinguished American films, Charles Laughton's *The Night of the Hunter* (1955) and Spike Lee's *Do the Right Thing* (1989), use the imagery of hands clenched into fists to illustrate the conflict between good and evil, between life and death. One hand is marked Love; the other, Hate. The tale of the hands, evoking an ancient biblical story, is a violent one; there is nothing in the framework of the story that envisions the power of Love, or goodness, as anything more than the ability to crush an opponent. In order to prevail, Love must resort to greater violence than Hate.

> Let me tell you the story of right hand, left hand. It's a tale of good and evil. Hate: it was with this hand that Cain iced his brother. Love: these five fingers, they go straight to the soul of man. The right hand: the hand of Love. The story of life is this: static. One hand is always fighting the other hand, and the left hand is kicking much ass. I mean, it looks like the right hand, Love, is finished. But hold on, stop the

presses, the right hand is coming back. Yeah, he got the left hand on the ropes now, that's right. Ooh, it's a devastating right, and Hate is hurt, he's down. Left-hand Hate KO'd by Love.

—Radio Raheem, in *Do the Right Thing*,
written, directed, and produced by Spike Lee,
in acknowledged homage to *The Night of the Hunter*

Drawing on these themes, *Considering Hate* proposes an alternative to this power struggle, offers an entirely new framework for the story, and calls for a new language with which to tell it.

1

DEHUMANIZATION AND VIOLENCE

"All paradises, all utopias, are designed by who is not there,
by the people who are not allowed in."

—TONI MORRISON

In the summer of 1955, Emmett Till, a fourteen-year-old black youth
from Chicago, was visiting relatives in Mississippi. In the company of
his cousin and friends, he went to a small grocery store to buy candy. A
white woman whose husband owned the store was the only employee
there. That night, acting on the belief that Till had insulted his wife,
the store owner and a friend abruptly awakened the sleeping youth in
the dark and kidnapped him. Three days later, Till's body was dragged
from the Tallahatchie River, weighted down with a seventy-four-pound
cotton-gin fan wrapped around his neck with barbed wire. Till had been
so savagely beaten before being shot in the head that he was identifiable
only by a ring on one finger. Like thousands of black people before him,
Emmett Till had been lynched.

When his body was returned to his mother, she chose an open casket,
permitting photographers, and the world, to witness the mutilation of her
son. The murder and subsequent celebratory acquittal of two killers by
an all-white, all-male jury galvanized the burgeoning African American

civil rights movement.[1] Decades later, Till's murder is described in contemporary terms as the hate crime that changed America.

HOW WE UNDERSTAND HATE VIOLENCE

Does the shift from "lynching" to "hate crime" matter? Yes, and for important reasons. Who is considered a valued part of the community, and who is considered expendable? Answering these questions requires examining the hate frame.

Think of a frame as a conceptual path shaping how people understand an issue and what ought to be done about it. The sleight-of-hand of the hate frame is that it invites people to believe the problem of violence directed against marginalized groups exists anywhere else but in themselves. The appeal of the hate frame is that it reaffirms a clear distinction between those who do violence and those who do not. For people not directly implicated in acts of hate violence, the distance between "us" and "them" feels secure.

Conceptualizing violence within the frame of hate makes it easy to mistake symptom for cause. Hatred is not the root cause of racism, misogyny, homophobia, violence against transgender people, violence against disabled people, or economic cruelty. Hate is a predictable consequence of deeply rooted, historically persistent forms of these maladies. They are foundational to institutionalizing hierarchies of power. Unnoticed and unexamined, they permeate mainstream culture.

Hate violence is also symbolic: it declares the superiority of one group of people over another. Those targeted are symbolically presented as psychically or physically disposable; the violence is a ritual of degradation. In 1998 in Jasper, Texas, James W. Byrd Jr., an African American, was tied to the back of a pickup truck by three white men, two of whom openly identified themselves as white supremacists, and dragged, still conscious, for three miles until one arm and his head were severed.

Proximity to such violence is terrifying. Society chooses to believe that only monsters and criminal bigots who exist beyond the pale of decency are capable of these things. Instinctively, people rush to morally distinguish themselves from those who commit such acts. The horror of this violence transforms into fear, rage, and desire for vengeance.

There are people who do not care that this violence occurs, and some who believe that the victims deserved or invited it. But many people, through mourning, remembering, and educating, register grief or anger. Some activists, seeking to deter hate violence, demand more policing and harsher sentencing. Many people offer support to the victims of violence and their families. "Stop Hate" rallies are organized and "This Is a Hate-Free Zone" posters appear. Initiatives teaching tolerance, prejudice reduction, and appreciation of diversity proliferate.

Despite these expressions of caring and conscience, hate violence remains part of the civic landscape. Many who are not touched by it assume that the notions of superiority and inferiority implicit to hate violence are so extreme that they are anathema to American society.

The irony is that they are not. The great successes of civil rights and social justice movements have not completely dislodged them. Hate violence is society's visible eruption of long-standing practices of injustice that are expressed in a multitude of ordinary ways. Like Poe's purloined letter, they are hidden in plain sight.

Murder is not the most common form of hate violence, although some groups such as people of color, and particularly transgender people of color, are at higher risk for being killed.[2] Assaults, rape, arson, bombing, verbal threats, intimidation, harassment, slurs, and the desecration of places of worship are more common. Yet it is the vivid act of killing, sometimes carried out with grotesque symbolism as in castration or dismemberment, that transfixes the public's imagination.

This is the public face of violence that is most likely to be condemned. Behind that façade are larger backdrops of dehumanizing violence. Transformative change can only occur by first understanding how hate violence is inextricably bound to broader social and political systems.

THROUGH THE LENS OF TWO "HATE CRIME" DEATHS

At first glance, Jennifer Daugherty, the thirty-year-old white woman with diminished mental capability, and Marcelo Lucero, the thirty-seven-year-old male Ecuadorian immigrant, had little in common except their murders, which were characterized by advocates as hate crimes.

In 2010 in Greensburg, Pennsylvania, Daugherty thought she was going to meet some friends. These "friends"—three women and three men—held Daugherty captive, raping and torturing her for two days before forcing her to write a suicide note and then stabbing her to death and dumping her body into a garbage can.

Two years earlier, in the Patchogue-Medford community on the eastern end of Long Island, Jeffrey Conroy, seventeen, white, an athlete at his local high school, and six of his friends (five of them white) went out looking "for Mexicans" to hurt. According to statements to police, they, like other youth in the area, had repeatedly engaged in "beaner hopping" but had never gotten in trouble. After firing BBs at one Latino man and beating another, they physically assaulted Marcelo Lucero and a companion who were walking down a street. As the other men attempted to escape, Conroy stabbed Lucero to death.[3]

It is ironic and sorrowful that the circumstances of their deaths, rather than their lives, highlight the humanity of Daugherty and Lucero in the public imagination. What does it mean to claim that this violence was caused by bias against disabled people and nonwhite immigrants, as if that bias were somehow anomalous? The deaths of Daugherty and Lucero were, tragically, foreseeable and, in some sense, inevitable. When public and private institutions regard some groups as inferior and possibly dangerous, discrimination and abuse is routinized through systemic beliefs and practices. This is the foundation for the violence, legal and extralegal, that inevitably ensues. Understanding how people with disabilities come to be dehumanized will illuminate its interdependent relationship with other forms of violence attributed to hate.

DEFORMING THE BODY POLITIC

Sociologist Robert Bogdan argues that how a society perceives people with disabilities has less to do with physiological or anatomical details "than with who we are culturally."[4]

In much of the Western world, disability has long been associated with the word *monster*. Derived from Latin, and meaning portent or warning, "monster" was historically used to describe a fetus or infant who was considered grotesque, with severe developmental abnormalities. Eventually the word became a warning that the "monster" was a threat to society. Theologians such as John Knox ("The First Blast of the Trumpet Against the Monstrous Regiment of Women," 1558) and political pamphleteers, including Edmund Burke and Thomas Paine, utilized "monstrosity" as a rhetorical device to signal what is deformed and to be feared, in contrast to what is presumed to be natural and virtuous. The language of monstrosity can be effectively adapted to almost any cultural context. The invocation of monstrosity "says nothing, or everything at once, all at a high pitch."[5]

"Monstrosity" declares that some people are intrinsically disfigured and therefore disfiguring. Thus, social well-being demands their identification, containment, and possibly, eradication. The United States has long used disability as a marker to define some as being outside the range of normalcy, decency, and qualification for citizenship.

The reality or metaphor of disability has been used to justify inequalities in changing social circumstances, and to legitimate the routinizing of inhumane and violent practices.[6] Simultaneously these commonly accepted practices have normalized violence against and even shifted blame onto those at whom they are directed.

This is evident in the popular nineteenth-century image of the vanishing Indian. The presumed racial inferiority of Native peoples justified policies that drove American Indian genocide. Contemporary newspapers condemned Native peoples as "barbarous savages" and invoked the classification of disability by labeling them an inferior species prone to disabling disease. This characterization made the case that the "savages" must be destroyed.[7] As scholar and activist Andrea Smith argues, much of this was connected to the fact that the conflation of Native bodies with filth and vermin connected them, in the colonial Christian mind, to sexual sin and perversity.[8]

This narrative justified governmental policies of removal and ultimately genocide. American Indians' "inevitable" disappearance would ensure, as a nineteenth-century Georgia newspaper correspondent declared, "that this beautiful country will now be prosperous and happy."[9]

The idea that the happiness and prosperity of some depends on the exclusion of others permeates American culture. To a significant degree, people define their own goodness and virtue by who they are not—a concept Toni Morrison efficiently sums up as "not-me."[10]

Disability powerfully influenced "three great citizenship debates of the nineteenth and early twentieth centuries":[11] the emancipation of black people, women's suffrage, and immigrant rights. In each of these debates, opponents of reform buttressed their arguments by imputing moral, intellectual, or physical impairments to those they wished to exclude.

The development in the late nineteenth and early twentieth centuries of a medical lexicon that articulated disability—*idiot, imbecile, moron, feebleminded, cretin, maniac, lunatic, cripple, degenerate, defective, delinquent, retardation*—as well as terms such as *freak, pinhead,* and *psycho* in popular culture—has had lasting cultural impact. Medicine and the social sciences have discarded these terms, but the words themselves continue to saturate public discourse.

In *Purity and Danger*, anthropologist Mary Douglas argues that the body is "a model which can stand for any bounded system. Its boundaries can represent any boundaries which are threatened or precarious."[12] How society regards bodies provides us with an image of society itself; this also allows us to see its fears and intentions of maintaining power hierarchies. Douglas believes the body "provides a basic scheme for all symbolism" and that most ideas about pollution of the larger social body "have some primary physiological reference."[13] Different kinds of bodies are branded with society's dichotomous ideas about fear and desire, guilt and innocence, goodness and evil, purity and pollution.

MANAGING DREAD

Philosopher Paul Ricoeur notes that "dread of the impure and rites of purification are in the background of all our feelings and all our behavior related to fault."[14] Dread of the polluting potential of the disabled body has deeply influenced US thought. Speaking at the National Conference of Charities and Correction in 1891, A. O. Wright, a Congregational minister and inspector of custodial and penal institutions in Wisconsin, characterized "the defective classes" as "a series of small, but very troublesome, tumors upon the body politic."[15]

Today Wright's statements are dismissed as ignorant and offensive. But this was in a period Mark Twain and Charles Dudley Warner described as the Gilded Age, a glittering façade of scientific and industrial progress that obscured poverty and injustice. In his time, A. O. Wright was in the mainstream of influential and respected reformers, scholars, scientists, and physicians.

These men and women saw their task as protecting the integrity and fitness of the nation by devising effective public responses to what they perceived to be issues of social degeneracy, including white anxieties following the abolition of slavery, massive migration from rural areas to large cities, immigration, labor unrest, growing poverty, and new ideas about women's sexual freedom. Their theories of degeneracy quickly translated this unease into medical prognoses, with profound social implications.

This dread of defilement, in conjunction with acknowledged or unconscious fear of symbolic filth, blocks an individual's ability to carefully reflect on one's life or actions.[16] Many people don't think about the ethical consequences of their actions; they just want to control their fear.

Metaphorical filth is also related to the fear of evil. Society engages in rites of purification to rid itself of this pollution—often through formal and informal policies of eradication or exclusion. Failing other solutions, A. O. Wright proclaimed, "We keep them shut up in institutions."[17]

Wright was prophetic. The United States has always locked up those thought to be degenerate or defective. This incarceration, coupled with isolation and impoverishment, has invariably led to abuse. By the mid-nineteenth century, reformers began exposing the inhumane conditions in poorhouses, jails, and prisons. Dorothea Dix, the most noted advocate for the humane, effective medical treatment of people with mental illness, described conditions in Illinois: "A helpless maniac confined throughout the bitter cold of winter to a dark and filthy pit. Prison inmates chained in hallways and cellars because no more men can be squeezed into the dank and airless cells. Aged paupers auctioned off by county officers to whoever will maintain them at the lowest cost."[18]

Early reformers regarded those considered insane or with cognitive disabilities as helpless individuals in need of public or privately funded residential care and education. Reform, however, can be a double-edged sword—particularly when it is implemented in ways that produce consequences the reformers did not originally intend.

Insane asylums, like prisons, became warehouses for people regarded as troublesome or undesirable. These were mostly white inmates; their counterparts among people of color were enslaved, in servitude, or in prisons. Many inmates simply did not conform to social norms or the accepted decorum. Madness had a moral as well as physiological etiology, and institutionalization was often regarded as proof of an individual's failure and lack of goodness.

As dominant culture found ways to hide people whose presence was disturbing, it simultaneously had a compulsion to stare, reimagining them as manifestations of its own terrors and desires. The advent of the mid-nineteenth-century's geographically isolated asylums coincided with the widespread popularity of a form of public amusement known as the sideshow.[19] Beginning in 1840, and for the next hundred years, sideshows affiliated with circuses, carnivals, and dime museums featured sensational displays of "freaks," industry shorthand for performers with unusual bodies—both real and cosmetically manufactured—and talents. These shows played to large audiences throughout America. The performers, whites as well as people of color, included conjoined twins, "half women/half men," hirsute women, little people, giants, "living skeletons," and people with microcephaly (a rare neuro-logical condition characterized by an extremely small head and limited cognitive development). Human beings exhibited in this way were of-ten falsely claimed to be from exotic, faraway cultures. Maximo and Bartola, two diminutive microcephalic children from Central America, were promoted in the mid-nineteenth century as "The Aztec Children," and later on, as adults, as "The Last of the Ancient Aztecs of Mexico."

These shows invited audiences to stare and be astonished, even dumbfounded, by the unexpected beings on display. Scientists gave their imprimaturs to deceptive claims, and they exploited performers as objects of study. The most infamous and best-known case concerns Saartje Baartman, a Khoisan woman taken from South Africa to Lon-don in the early nineteenth century. Displayed seminude as "the Hot-tentot Venus" in sideshows throughout Great Britain and Europe, she became an involuntary object of medical study, made to represent rac-ist concepts of black female sexuality.[20]

Audiences were undoubtedly reassured of what they assumed to be their own racial and physiological normality. A commercial enterprise, the sideshow allowed people to ignore harsher offstage realities. In the American imagination, disabled people had long been seen as objects of contempt and pity. By the late nineteenth century, they also became an embodiment of menace.

Thirty years after the implementation of reforms such as therapeu-tic treatment and moral instruction came the birth of eugenics, or "the science of good breeding." This paved the way for the creation of the pseudoscientific category of the born criminal. Eugenicists quickly de-veloped initiatives for the social and biological removal of defectives from the national body.[21]

In America, criminality had always been linked to indigenous peo-ples, blacks, and poor people. Now people with particular disabilities were targeted. Individuals with psychiatric and cognitive disorders, physically disabling conditions such as epilepsy, and catchall fictions such as moral insanity (the appearance of normal intelligence combined with an inability to distinguish right from wrong; altruism was seen as a variant of moral insanity), were added to the criminal mix.

THE BODY REVEALS DANGER AND DEFILEMENT

Drawing on the pseudoscientific fields of phrenology, the study of the shape of the skull, and physiognomy, the analysis of facial features and expressions, the new academic field of criminology literally "read" the body for external evidence of innate criminality. Between 1876 and 1897, Italian physician Cesare Lombroso produced five editions of his signature work, *Criminal Man*, the first in-depth, purportedly scientific discussion advancing the theory of the born criminal.[22] *Criminal Woman* appeared in 1893.[23] Lombroso invented a classification system in which Caucasian heterosexual men without a discernible disability stood at the apex of virtue. Born criminals, by contrast, included all people of color and various white ethnic groups classified as atavistic throwbacks to primitive violent cultures. Though inferior to men, women were seen as less inclined to criminality, except for those drawn to prostitution or having "mannish" features and behaviors, a code for lesbians. These ideas were incorporated into standard texts in medicine and the social sciences, often with drawings and photographs that reinforced a certain view of the physical characteristics deemed to reveal criminality. The influence of these ideas was enormous. As the science behind them was discredited, "born criminal" theories gave way to a new phantom menace: the psychopath. Yet public-policy measures created to contain and eradicate the born criminal continue to cast profound shadows over contemporary discussions about crime, punishment, and justice.

The US population has grown in four ways: slavery, annexation and colonization, immigration, and reproduction.[24] In his 1916 jeremiad *The Passing of the Great Race*, conservationist and naturalist Madison Grant proposed "a rigid system of selection" that would eliminate presumptive social failures. He advocated "beginning always with the criminal, the diseased and the insane," and expanding the system from there to perhaps include "worthless race types."[25] This was a biologized interpretation of manifest destiny.[26] Grant reserved his deepest contempt for black people, but bewailed the threatening influence of Jews and Mexicans as well as Slavs, Muslims, and Asians.

Scientific racism was the bleak heart of the American eugenics movement. This crusade claimed ownership of bodies, lives, public spaces, even individual and collective biological futures. It did not create new ideas about race, ethnicity, gender, class, disability, or citizenship so much as promote its supremacist ideology within a purportedly objective, evidence-based discussion.

The United States had historically attempted to control Native peoples and their reproduction through genocide. "Kill them all, big and small. Nits make lice," Colonel John Chivington of the territorial Colorado Volunteers is reported to have said in justifying an 1864 cavalry massacre of peaceful Cheyenne and Arapaho people, primarily women and children, camped in southeastern Colorado. And the fact that children born to black women were the property of slaveholders, observes historian Dorothy Roberts, "made control of reproduction a central aspect of whites' subjugation of African people in America."[27]

Immigrants whose origins were anathema to eugenicists posed special challenges. In his best-selling *The Rising Tide of Color Against White World-Supremacy* (1920), Lothrop Stoddard viewed immigration restrictions as an essential large-scale intervention "by which inferior stocks can be prevented from both diluting and supplanting good stock. Just as we isolate bacterial invasions, and starve out the bacteria by limiting the area and amount of their food-supply, so we can compel an inferior race to remain in its habitat."[28]

Nativism—hostile beliefs directed by white American people at the foreign-born—took deeper root, inflamed by fears that immigrants were responsible for outbreaks of disease. This "medicalization of pre-existing nativist prejudices," historian of science Alan M. Kraut writes, "occurs when the justification for excluding members of a particular group includes charges that they constitute a health menace and may endanger their hosts."[29] At different historical moments Chinese immigrants were blamed for an outbreak of bubonic plague, Jewish immigrants for tuberculosis, and more recently, Haitians and foreign-born gay men for HIV/AIDS. Susan Sontag observes that this stigmatization wrongly conflates disease with identity, with the result that people who are ill are dehumanized and exposed to harassment.[30]

Eugenics articulated and solidified a social template for human triage that led to new laws further limiting those seen as contaminating influences. This continued an American tradition of creating statutes to reduce the presence of "undesirables" in the public sphere. Among them were post-abolition Black Codes criminalizing black people for ordinary activities that were entirely legal for whites, and similar laws for American Indians. California's 1855 Anti-Vagrancy Act singled out "all persons who are commonly known as 'Greasers' or the issue of Spanish or Indian blood." Other vaguely worded and selectively enforced laws criminalized such behaviors as "strolling or wandering about" and "loitering."

Starting in the late nineteenth century, a series of codes—collectively termed "ugly laws" by disability activists—were enacted in various municipalities. One such ordinance provided a penalty for the public visibility of "any person who is diseased, maimed, mutilated, or in any way deformed, so as to be an unsightly or disgusting object, or an improper person to be allowed in or on the streets, highways, thoroughfares, or public places."

Ugly laws directly targeted poor people with disabilities who begged or solicited, since, although the law was neutrally worded, only the poor were cited. The laws also ignored causes of many disabilities: intimate (domestic) violence, war, and industrial injuries. People of color were treated more harshly than poor whites, and "[a] tensely conjoined mixture of ableism, biologized racism, and nativism emerged in American culture," equating the concepts of unsightliness, begging, and "alien."[31] Ugly laws no longer exist, but they foreshadowed contemporary municipal statutes that criminalize homeless people, many of whom have disabilities.

The same anxieties were institutionalized in laws governing immigration and citizenship. From 1790 to the post–Civil War era, only those who were free, white, and had resided in the United States for a specified number of years could be naturalized. In the late nineteenth and early twentieth centuries, those suffering the most restrictive and exclusionary impacts were Chinese and Japanese laborers, as well as certain categories of people from southern and southeastern Asia and from southern and eastern Europe.

The militarization of the US-Mexico border began in the early twentieth century and expanded in 1924 with the creation of the US Border Patrol. During the Great Depression, immigration authorities launched raids on Mexican American communities in California, Arizona, and Texas, forcibly deporting more than 400,000 people without due process, many of whom were citizens born in the United States.

All such measures do enormous violence to the concept of the Commons, which has existed in different cultural iterations throughout the world for centuries. This refers to those resources—social, cultural, ecological, and spatial—that are held in common by, shared, and accessible to all members of a society. The Commons, by its very nature, is communal because certain elements—such as clean air and water, the ability to move freely in society, and housing, education, and health care—are essential to the creation of community and should be shared. Increasingly, dominant American culture has sought to enclose the Commons and reserve its gifts for only a few.

POLICING THE BIOLOGICAL FUTURE

The tactical capstone of the American eugenics movement was the enactment, in a majority of states, of compulsory or coercive sterilization laws. These targeted poor people, people of color, people with certain disabilities, prisoners, and anyone considered undesirable (homosexuals among them). People in all of these categories were presumed to have uncontrollable, unpredictable, or abnormal sexual impulses.

Carrie Buck, a young white woman from Virginia, was eighteen years old when selected under a state statute mandating the sterilization of "mental defectives." Buck was classified as a feebleminded moral delinquent prone to sexual misconduct because she had borne a child out of wedlock. In 1927 in *Buck v. Bell*, the US Supreme Court upheld the statute, rejecting the argument that it denied Buck the right to due process and equal protection of the laws under the Fourteenth Amendment. The ruling, which still stands, was announced by Supreme Court justice Oliver Wendell Holmes Jr.: "It is better for all the world if instead of waiting to execute degenerate offspring for crime, or to let them starve for their imbecility, society can prevent those who are manifestly unfit from continuing their kind." Much later, close review of the records determined that the case against Carrie Buck was a legal sham. She was neither feebleminded nor guilty of sexual misconduct; her pregnancy was the result of sexual assault. Between 1907 and 1937, more than sixty thousand involuntary sterilizations were performed in the United States.[32] Many others, never recorded, were performed in hospitals, asylums, or prisons, or in states that kept no records.

American initiatives galvanized global interest in eugenics and provided a model for compulsory sterilization initiatives in Germany, Canada, Switzerland, Sweden, Japan, and other countries. In Germany, over 400,000 sterilizations were performed under the authority of a 1933 law instituted by Adolf Hitler to prevent "hereditarily diseased off-spring." During the 1945–1947 trials for crimes against humanity, Nazi physicians defended their involvement in mass sterilization, medical experimentation, and euthanasia programs by citing *Buck v. Bell*.

Though most compulsory sterilization laws were eventually re-pealed, the practice continued. Between 1950 and 1968, more than one-third of all women of childbearing age in Puerto Rico were steril-ized. During the 1960s and 1970s, 100,000 to 150,000 poor women in the South, half of them black and some as young as twelve, were coerced or manipulated into consenting to sterilization. At the same time in California, low-income migrant Latinas were sterilized without their consent or with coerced consent during Caesarian section. In the 1970s, physicians at Indian Health Service (IHS) and other contracted health facilities performed thousands of sterilizations on Native women of childbearing age. Independent studies claim that 25 to 50 percent of all Native women of childbearing age were affected. According to the Center for Investigative Reporting, between 2006 and 2010, at least 148 women in California prisons were sterilized under coercive conditions, without the state's approval.[33]

ENDURING ETHICS OF EXCLUSION AND EXPENDABILITY

Despite reforms, or in some cases because of them, deplorable treatment of human beings remains an entrenched part of the American institutional mainstream.

Harassment and assaults directed at Latinos were common in Suffolk County, New York, when Marcelo Lucero was killed in 2008. Over the decades, a growing influx of immigrants had been met by increased xenophobia. Political leaders actively sought the help of anti-immigration organizations to advise them on public policy. Most people in the local community supported the enactment of laws that accelerated the criminalization of Latinos. Verbal and physical harassment of Latinos was commonplace. In 2007 county executive Steve Levy, a vociferous proponent of anti-immigrant measures, was re-elected with 96 percent of the vote.

When Lucero was killed, Levy blamed it all on white supremacists and bad people. The murder of Lucero turned a harsh and unwelcome spotlight on xenophobic tensions and became a catalyst for some change. A broad range of community organizations and social justice advocates stood together, and when Levy left office, his administration was replaced with one determined to foster a less hostile environment. Because Lucero's murder was attributed to irrational bias, and not larger, structural problems, little deep change occurred, though with diligent, ongoing effort, greater transformation may be possible. The hostility that led to his death had been nurtured for well over a century by the legacy of a US war waged against Mexico, generations of eugenic ideology, anxieties about legal and unauthorized immigration, job losses, economic hard times, and rising fears about terrorism and border security.

This anxiety and resentment is embodied in the militarized US-Mexico border, contributing to dominant American ideas about criminality and nonwhiteness. Hundreds of miles of fences have been erected, while electronic sensors, twenty thousand members of the US Border Patrol, satellites, helicopters, and other aircraft, including drones, keep watch.

The same fears have driven the explosive growth of immigrant detention, which mushroomed in 1996 during the Clinton administration, and again after 9/11. Being in the United States without appropriate authorization is a civil, not a criminal infraction. Nevertheless, each year 300,000 to 400,000 immigrants are held in hundreds of facilities, ranging from local and county jails (with federal contracts) to detention centers resembling prisons. Under contract with US Immigration and Customs Enforcement (ICE), private, for-profit corporations administer many of these facilities.

Immigrant detention is a lucrative industry, driven by get-tough laws.[34] In the years following 9/11, Congress established a statutory "detention bed quota" that increased over time. By 2013 the federal government was required to detain at least thirty-four thousand people per day, most of whom are Latino. In 2010 Arizona became the first state to intensify the criminalization of immigrants by enacting Senate Bill (SB) 1070. Though the wording is race-neutral, this was primarily targeted at Latinos as well as people of Asian descent and anyone else presumed to be "foreign." The law requires police, acting on a "reasonable suspicion" that a person who is stopped is not legally authorized to be in the United States, to determine the immigration status of that person. Because it is based entirely on how a person looks or sounds, the statute institutionalizes racial profiling. And in many cases, detention is mandatory, especially for people with prior (often minor) criminal records, even when they have already been released by the criminal legal system. By 2014 five other states—Alabama, Georgia, Indiana, South Carolina, and Utah—had adopted similar laws, all of which fuel detention.

In this system detention becomes preemptive punishment. Since proceedings to determine immigrant status are civil, detainees have no right to publicly funded legal representation. Only those who can afford private attorneys, or manage to locate the rare free legal service provider, have counsel. José Antonio Franco-Gonzales, twenty-nine years old, Mexican, and the son of lawful permanent residents, was detained between 2005 and 2010 without access to an attorney or a hearing to determine if his continuing detention was justifiable. A judge had closed his case on the grounds that the young man, who had a severe cognitive disability, was not mentally capable of understanding the proceedings. Yet authorities continued to move Franco-Gonzales from one Southern California detention facility to another until the American Civil Liberties Union (ACLU) intervened.

Detention as a solution for social tensions is not only for immigrants. In the 1950s the advent of antipsychotic medications allowed many people with severe forms of mental illness to be deinstitutionalized. The reforms were accelerated in the 1960s by a series of exposés of inhumane conditions in asylums and psychiatric hospitals and again in the 1970s and 1980s by states that seized on an opportunity to slash human needs spending. Predictably, resources promised for community-based treatment programs never materialized, and increased homelessness and poverty accompanied mass deinstitutionalization.

The political solution completely reversed the Dorothea Dix reforms that, 170 years earlier, had released (white) people with mental illness from the nation's jails, prisons, and poorhouses and revamped hospitals into institutions with, at least at the beginning, more humane intentions. The late-twentieth-century choice, by contrast, was the result of accepting, without debate, America's default option: imprisonment. Today, American prisons and jails are the major institutions housing people with mental illness. In 2006 the Bureau of

Justice Statistics estimated that more than half of the 2.3 million people then incarcerated in US prisons and jails suffered from diagnosed mental health problems, a substantial percentage of them experiencing schizophrenia or bipolar disorder. Violence is commonplace in these facilities; guards and staff are not equipped to provide appropriate and humane treatment. Medications are often denied, and extended solitary confinement, sometimes extending for years, even decades, is routine. The adverse neural and psychological impacts of long-term isolation have been well documented: mental illnesses grow worse, and prisoners considered "healthy" easily descend into psychosis, self-harm, and suicide.[35]

Reforms, such as the 1990 Americans with Disabilities Act (ADA), have fared better, though the ADA continues to come under attack. The act prohibits discrimination in employment, government services, public accommodations, commercial facilities, and transportation. The ADA does not simply ban discrimination but requires reasonable structural changes and support, making possible tangible, constructive changes in people's lives.

After its passage, significant anti-ADA backlash quickly emerged. Editorial cartoons mocked the law; a popular image portrayed the ADA as mandating the hiring of insane people. Opponents argued that the law is unfair to business owners. In 1999 the US Supreme Court invalidated part of the ADA as it applied to states, and in other decisions further limited the reach of the law. Efforts continue today to weaken it still more.

The necessity for the ADA, as well as problems inherent in its enforcement, is evident in the experiences of men who worked for Henry's Turkey Service, a labor broker headquartered in Texas. Beginning in the 1960s, and for forty years, hundreds of men with cognitive disabilities, many of them people of color, were discharged from a state institution into "rehabilitative" work for the company. The men dispatched to labor camps in six states, including one in Atalissa, Iowa, constituted an easily exploitable workforce. Paid sixty-five dollars a month, if at all, they received inadequate health care. They were housed in an old, cockroach-infested bunkhouse whose doors were locked at night. Many of the men were physically abused. As a result of persistent investigative reporting by the *Des Moines Register*, the state fire marshal closed down the bunkhouse in 2009. Some of the men, who had been assigned numbers but possessed no legal form of personal identification, had been there for decades.

Many people knew of these conditions over the course of four decades but did nothing. The few who did protest found that their complaints to state and federal agencies were ignored or resulted in only one-time remedies. Only when the *Des Moines Register* pursued the story, at the behest of one worker's sister, did federal and state agencies take concerted action.

By 2013, as a result of legal action pursued by the federal Equal Employment Opportunity Commission, jurors awarded each Henry's Turkey Service worker $7.5 million for a total of $240 million, an amount later slashed because it exceeded a federal cap on jury awards, based on the number of people affected. The company accrued additional federal and state judgments: civil penalties, payment for back wages, and administrative fines. By 2014 authorities faced difficulties collecting the money.

Federal and state officials claim that a clear message has been sent, and that the dignity of the workers has been validated. The Iowa attorney general did not file criminal charges, asserting that accountability would best be achieved via fines and penalties.[36]

THE ALCHEMY OF VIOLENCE

It is difficult for people to bear witness to violence attributed to hate. It is even much harder for many to acknowledge the broader patterns of violence and suffering. And it is still more painful to acknowledge the interdependent nature of hate violence and broader systems of power.

In *The Iliad, or the Poem of Force* (1940), Simone Weil examines that connection, writing that the true subject of Homer's epic work is force and "the human spirit . . . as modified by its relations with force."

For Weil, force is "that x that turns anybody who is subjected to it into a thing." She is not claiming that an intrinsic humanity is destroyed, but that those wielding force have already refused to recognize this humanity. In its ultimate, logical form, force creates corpses. Before physical death, it delivers people into a civil death: their abilities to think, feel, hope, create, love, experience pain, and suffer loss have already ceased to exist in the eyes of those who wield this force. At the heart of it is "that marvelous indifference that the strong feel toward the weak."[37]

The essence of such disregard is captured brilliantly in Franz Kafka's "The Bucket Rider," written after the author lived through a harsh winter in Berlin. In the story, a poor man, whose coal bucket is empty, will freeze to death unless he obtains fuel. Riding his bucket like a steed, he goes to the coal dealer and knocks at the door, pleading. While he cannot pay "just yet," he has been a loyal customer and is deserving of just the smallest kindness. The coal dealer's wife answers the door; frozen tears dimming his eyes, the poor man begs to be seen and heard: "I beg you, just a shovelful. . . . One shovelful of the worst you have." The woman refuses to see, even to acknowledge, his desperate plea. "I see nothing, I hear nothing," she tells her husband. With a wave of her apron and a brandishing of her fist, she shoos away the Bucket

Rider—the still-living human who, in this instant, is being erased. The door to the shop closes, and the shivering man, astride his bucket, will "ascend into the regions of the ice mountains," already lost forever.

Indifference produces violence. As Kafka's tale illustrates, it is indifference, which may or may not involve hatred, that imposes the death sentence. These two concepts—indifference to the humanity of the Other, and the use of force that turns the Other into a thing—illuminate the interdependent nature of many forms of violence.

Another disquieting question arises: What if sensational acts of hate violence, which media accounts often represent as aberrant, actually reflect existing community norms?

This depends on how people understand violence. Have they personally experienced the coercive force that turns people into things? Are they willing to step beyond their own experiences and listen to, even believe, others whose experiences and histories are different?

In *Violence*, philosopher Slavoj Zizek writes about broader forms of subjugation: "We're talking here of the violence inherent in a system: not only direct physical violence, but also the more subtle forms of coercion that sustain relations of domination and exploitation, including the threat of violence."[38]

This violence, which is so deeply embedded in "business as usual," is never acknowledged as such by those who benefit from it economically, socially, politically, or religiously. It arises from "often unconscious assumptions and reactions of well-meaning people in ordinary interactions."[39] Simply put, injustice and violence arise from a totality of conventional actions, beliefs, policies, and practices that degrade others, even when there is no conscious intention to do violence to an entire segment of the population. It doesn't take monsters to inflict terrible injury.

CULTURES OF VIOLENCE

The very idea of violence raises important questions that are never asked openly in policy discussions. What constitutes humanity? Whose lives are considered worthy of justice, dignity, and compassion? Whose lives are considered inferior, disposable? Why? Who has the power to make and enforce these judgments? The answers are not always clear, and certainly not found in the legal system. These questions go directly to the heart of that which is commonplace—story lines and images in mass media, popular culture, institutional policies and practices, and personal and group behaviors that normalize, excuse, or deny common forms of violence—even as those same forms of violence are legally proscribed.

In the United States, rape, sexual assault, child sexual abuse, coercion, and harassment are subject to criminal prosecution, including prosecution as a hate crime. These legal remedies, though seldom pursued, support the idea that American society does not tolerate this violence. Furthermore, people believe that sexual crimes are not tolerated because, in the public imagination, rape symbolizes the violation of all that is innocent. In its common form the rape story becomes an idealized tale of public virtue and individualized evil.

Reality reveals this to be untrue. This idealized concept of justice coexists with a rape culture in which sexual violence is tolerated as an everyday aspect of private and public life. Rape culture is defined by attitudes and cultural messages that continually downplay the extent of sexual violence, stigmatize those who are assaulted, and celebrate male sexual aggression. When rape culture is acknowledged at all, it is often described as a violent form of sexism that affects all women equally. That is a simplification and a distortion.

Andrea Smith, noting the centrality of sexual violence to colonial conquest, argues that it is "a tool by which certain peoples become marked as inherently 'rapable.'"[40] Rape can be and often is a weapon used to enforce racial, gender, and economic power differences. To focus on an individual act of rape obscures the understanding that sexual violence often "encompasses a wide range of strategies designed . . . to destroy peoples [and] their sense of being a people."[41] For most of US history, the law did not recognize the rape of black women as a crime. An analysis of rape that focuses only on individual crimes produces the archetypal rapist: the black man, violent thug, stranger, and interloper with uncontrollable sexual appetites: the mythic defiler-of-white-innocence. This image was used to justify lynching and today continues to influence prosecutorial decisions.[42] The archetypal rapist takes other forms in the public imagination: the dangerous stranger, the dangerous date, and the unknown lurker who inhabits dark alleys. The reality is that most attackers are known to those whom they assault, are familiar community figures, or occupy positions of responsibility.

From time to time, a horrific act of sexual violence galvanizes the public conscience. In New Delhi, India in 2012, a twenty-three-year-old physical therapy student and her male companion boarded a bus. The driver, several other adult men, and a youth brutally beat the couple, raped the woman, and then penetrated her body with an iron rod before throwing her and her companion, both naked, from the bus. She died some days later; he survived. The nightmarish nature of the rape and murder gave rise to protests against sexual violence in India and against the failure of the police and legal system to address the problem. Death sentences were given to the adult perpetrators with the assurance that the severity of sentencing proved that India took sexual violence against women seriously. Yet gang rapes, sometimes combined with murder, continue.

Around the same time, American activists were also denouncing legal and societal failures to address sexual violence. Multiple news reports appeared—about the Steubenville case and others—in which young white women were raped by at least one, usually several, young men who were classmates or friends of the women. Not surprisingly, there is a notable absence of reports about the experiences of women of color in these mainstream rape narratives. Bystanders witnessed the assaults, but did nothing to stop or report them. The media, community members, police, and even some of their friends held the women accountable because of their excessive drinking; the young men were not held accountable. Photographs, videos, and texts distributed via cell phones and social media amplified the assaults and exposed the young women to harassment. Law enforcement actions were hesitant and inconsistent. In some cases, serious community rifts opened, centered on contested ideas of innocence, guilt, consent, and morality. At the heart of these divisions was the belief that the accused were not criminal types, so the immorality must be located entirely in the young women.

Rape is imagined as an unspeakable crime, an affront to decency, perpetrated by violent interlopers. The reality is that it is an ordinary and integral part of everyday life.

An exhaustive 2010 federal study conducted by the National Center for Injury Prevention and Control at the Centers for Disease Control and Prevention estimated that almost 20 percent of women have been raped or experienced attempted rape in their lifetime. Scandals involving inadequate institutional responses to allegations of sexual harassment and assault regularly erupt in places considered to be respectable, including public and private universities—only to be downplayed or covered up by responsible people in positions of power. In 2013 the Pentagon estimated that at least twenty-six thousand sexual assaults had occurred in the US armed forces in the preceding year. Between 1950 and 2010, there were at least 10,667 individual reports that an estimated 4,000 priests in the US Catholic Church had sexually abused minors.[43] Scandals have also erupted in other faith communities, including Buddhist, Jewish, Muslim, and various Protestant Christian denominations.

In US jails, prisons, immigrant detention centers, and juvenile corrections centers, multiple forms of sexual abuse are so pervasive as to be considered a form of punishment. Prisoners commit sexual violence against their peers, but most abuse is perpetrated by correctional staff.[44] Sexual violence continues to be a common feature of US policing, and, as the photographs of torture and sexual humiliation of prisoners held at Abu Ghraib show us, and other reports confirm, sexualized torture and humiliation permeate the "war on terror."

Myths and distortions have come to define hate, violence, and justice in the public imagination. Most politicians have a strongly vested interest in not rocking the boat by telling the truth. The discussions that shape public understanding of these concepts are not exclusively political. Many people just want to locate the problem out there and with somebody else.

In some sense, the problem *is* also out there. It is in the stories we see in films, in novels, on television. Something else beyond political analysis is at work, operating as images, myths, symbols, archetypes, and story. This is the popular culture that permeates American society and sneaks into the psyche, often quietly and deeply, in ways that are seldom consciously noted.

2

HATE IN THE PUBLIC IMAGINATION

"Everything is held together with stories."
—BARRY LOPEZ

Popular culture profoundly shapes how we think about justice, goodness, and fairness; its messages change over time. Movies, television, magazines, news reporting, and music are lenses through which we understand and teach basic ideas about these concepts. Even a brief survey of hate and justice in film is revealing.

Ideas about hatred and what should be done about it in Hollywood films are a reflection of Americans' fears, hopes, and expectations about power, race, gender, and sexuality. Films display the best and the worst impulses of American culture, often conflicting with one another in the same narrative.

Embedded in this history is a common theme of the struggle between the individual and oppressive social systems. There is no set pattern here. Films portray both individuals and social systems as bad or good. Audiences view these fluid and shifting positions according to their own political beliefs and experiences. Representation is not the same as articulated political ideology. Art is often indirect and frequently messy; great art often provides us with more food for thought, not less; more ways to see the world, not a limited one. At its most provocative and best, popular culture can do this as well. Film narratives focus on individual characters, and representations of hate and violence often do not present audiences with a larger analysis.

VISUALIZING HATE AND JUSTICE IN EARLY HOLLYWOOD

The birth of the American film industry, first in New York and then Hollywood, changed how Americans thought about politics, law, and social justice. Beginning in colonial times, newspapers, pamphlets, and books were enormously influential in shaping public opinion. They helped formulate ideas about justice and helped an ever-growing reading population to engage in public conversations about ethics and morality. Images played a large part in this (think of the illustrations of abused slaves in abolitionist literature), and the advent of photography in the mid-nineteenth century radically transformed the cultural influence of images.

Susan Sontag argues in *On Photography* that the photograph's power is that it provides evidence: "Something we hear about, but doubt, seems proven when we are shown a photograph."[1] The potential for photograph-as-evidence to incite moral outrage is great, although it may be one of numerous responses. Matthew Brady's photographs of the Civil War dead in mass graves produced moral outrage at war, sadness, or even a further incitement to fight. Sontag notes that "what determines the possibility of being affected morally by photographs is the existence of relevant political consciousness."[2] Images do not exist outside of a political context.

The relationship between an image and moral judgment was complicated by the motion picture. Large numbers of people could be powerfully influenced, as a group, by viewing moving images that conveyed messages through emotional and psychological narratives. Even as they understood images were staged and edited to create a narrative, audiences experienced the images as physical and moral evidence. While the interpretation of images was shaped by each individual's preexisting political consciousness, films contained the potential to stimulate question about and to shape individuals' perceptions of how power shaped human and social relationships.

The American film industry began in the 1890s and quickly captured the country's imagination. One of the first films to be publicly screened was William Heise's *The Kiss* (1896). The forty-seven-second reenactment, from a Broadway play, of a heterosexual kiss was frequently banned, because evidence of this up-close intimacy was considered indecent. (Three decades later the motion picture industry, under pressure from organized religion, would begin to censor itself.) In 1903, Edwin S. Porter's *The Great Train Robbery*, a twelve-minute narrative with a plot, often called the first silent movie, presented audiences with what were to become salient themes in Hollywood films: greed, robbery, violence, murder, and vigilante justice. These two films set the standard for what audiences loved in films—what critic Pauline Kael insisted was the enduring appeal of movies captured in the phrase "kiss-kiss bang-bang"—sex and action.[3]

Sex and action exist in narratives, and in 1915 D. W. Griffith's *The Birth of a Nation* produced a politically fraught public discussion of hate, race, power, and sex. This was a sprawling film, three hours and ten minutes long, that celebrated the birth of the Ku Klux Klan in the South during Reconstruction. *The Birth of a Nation*'s complicated plot involved Northern and Southern families with overlapping romantic interactions, abolition, duplicitous freed slaves, rape, miscegenation, and a "happy ending" in which freed slaves are prevented from voting by the Klan. The recently formed NAACP protested the film's jubilant depiction of race hatred, and riots broke out in several cities where the film was shown. The themes of predatory black male sexuality and voter suppression resonate today, but the more lasting message of the film is the idea that justice can only be found by "taking it into your own hands."

The Birth of a Nation spoke to and inflamed racial tensions in the early twentieth century. It also resonated with the evolving tensions around immigration, since some immigrants—Irish, Italians, and eastern European Jews among them—were not considered culturally or racially white. American individualism dominated public discourse about immigration, and the narrative of the Klan's violently righting the injustices of Reconstruction dovetailed with long-standing ideas about American individualism.

Between 1890 and 1920, thirteen million immigrants from northern and southern Europe arrived in the United States. Welcomed as the new pilgrims and embraced by industrialists as cheap labor, immigrants lived in cities across the United States. Caught in a vortex of conflicting enactments of American individualism, they were told they could succeed through hard work, even though they were persecuted, sometimes violently, as intrusive foreigners by nativist groups including the Ku Klux Klan. The quest for extralegal justice is at the heart of American individualism in *The Birth of a Nation* and provides a template for the hate frame.

The Birth of a Nation set one standard for how movie audiences imagined and internally negotiated violence and justice. Other films took a very different view. Hollywood produced numerous films (most of them now forgotten) about the hardships immigrants faced in their new homeland. E. Mason Hopper's feature-length *Hungry Hearts* (1922) is based on Polish-Jewish immigrant Anzia Yezierska's short stories. Yezierska so defined the New York immigrant experience that producer Samuel Goldwyn, himself an immigrant, immediately bought the rights to her novels and stories. Her instant success earned her the title "the ghetto Cinderella."[4]

In *Hungry Hearts* a poor immigrant Jewish woman, who supports her family by taking in laundry, works ceaselessly to fix up and paint her apartment and make it, literally, *white*. When she succeeds, her assimilated Jewish landlord, claiming the apartment is now worth more, raises the rent. Unable to pay, she is threatened with eviction. In a fury she destroys the kitchen with an ax and is brought to court. The gentile judge finds her not guilty and argues that in America no one should be exploited. At the close of the film the woman and her family move to a country cottage with a white picket fence, and her daughter marries the lawyer who represented them in court. (In Yezierska's story the woman becomes homeless.)

Hungry Hearts, catering to an immigrant audience eager to see their lives *and* their dreams on the screen, is typical of films that acknowledged immigrant hardships and provided happy endings. *The Birth of a Nation* predicates injustice based upon race—and reverses who is oppressed. *Hungry Hearts* ignores racism and focuses on poverty and economic justice. Utilizing political archetypes—the landlord is bad because he is a landlord; the judge is good because he is an American judge—the film presents an idealized notion of American justice, based on the idea that social roles dictate individual values, that is as seamless as it is unrealistic. This vision of justice, incongruent with the realities of American racism and economic disadvantage, remained a constant in American film.

These ideas of justice were, by and large, about citizens who were considered "white," including in the rare films that dealt with anti-Semitism such as Mervyn LeRoy's *They Won't Forget* (1937), which was based on the 1915 lynching of Leo Frank, a Jew. African American characters, presented as domestics or porters, were always peripheral to a central white narrative. James Whale's *Showboat* (1936) displayed glimmers of a more sophisticated understanding of racial animus, but its radical potential was overwhelmed by the use of racial stereotypes and narrative that ultimately focused on white characters. Between 1915 and 1950 a small, vibrant industry consisted of "race films" produced or directed by and starring African Americans. Approximately five hundred feature-length and short films were made for and played almost exclusively to black audiences. Oscar Micheaux's *Within Our Gates* (1919), for example, dealt with the revival of the Ku Klux Klan, lynching, mixed-race African Americans, and the education of black children. Overwhelmingly, and up until the early 1960s, Hollywood films represented and reinforced the realities of segregation.

DEPRESSION JUSTICE

Within this context of racial exclusion, films of the Depression brought ideas about justice and goodness, and the possibility of acting for the good of others, into sharper focus. Bolstered by Roosevelt's New Deal, films increasingly focused on social justice issues and received increasing popular support.

This presentation of ethical societal themes arose from a combination of American populism and individualism. The stock market crash of 1929 devastated most Americans. In response, films offered narratives of personal and social redemption rooted in the goodness of American life and a belief in the democratic system. Arguing that Americans were all in this together, the narratives nonetheless avoided any discussion of collective responsibility for change. Justice was achieved through the actions and bravery of the extraordinary common man. Frank Capra's *Mr. Deeds Goes to Town* (1936) and *Mr. Smith Goes to Washington* (1939) praise the decency of the mythical average American who, like Mr. Deeds, does not care about money or, like

Mr. Smith, fights greed-fueled political corruption. Wealth is rejected in favor of real values. The fantasy here, in a country filled with impoverished people, was that you did not need money to be a real or good American.

The imagined relationship of justice and goodness emerges from a concept of citizenship that is completely white and predicated on a vaguely classless America. These films argue that if the people in charge would just be decent, there would be no injustice. Here goodness resides in a beleaguered, but always triumphant, American everyman whose innocence is threatened by corrupt political power and money. Realistically, power and money can corrupt. But these films do not provide an analysis of how corruption occurs, or how it can be changed from within or outside of the system.

The hard-edged, realistic crime and prison films of the period contradicted this. These films, enormously popular, explicitly critiqued American social structures that led to criminal behavior and exposed judicial punishment and the prison system. William Wyler's *Dead End* (1937) provided an excoriating look at how urban poverty bred crime and destroyed any possibility of the elusive American dream embodied in Frank Capra's films. Michael Curtiz's *20,000 Years in Sing Sing* (1932) and Mervyn LeRoy's *I Am a Fugitive from a Chain Gang* (1932) were sympathetic narratives of guilty and innocent men trapped in unethical, crushing criminal legal systems.

Gangsters often became antiheroes. Mervyn LeRoy's *Little Caesar* (1931), loosely based on the career of Al Capone, glamorized but did not valorize its lead character. Though he was punished at the film's end, many audiences viewed his antisocial impulses as positive traits. Crime films, depicting a deeper understanding of how social systems worked, were realistic representations of people's lives: brutal, unfair, and often inescapable. Their emphasis was on the disenfranchisement of the group by the legal and economic system rather than the empowerment of the individual within it.

These films are animated by a concept of injustice produced not by individuals, but by economic inequality and corrupt law enforcement. The films easily generate sympathy for the victimized little man. In Fritz Lang's *You Only Live Once* (1937), Eddie and Joan Taylor, based on Bonnie and Clyde, are a doomed couple, victimized by injustice, on the run from the law. The films are rarely hopeful, and there is little chance for the cycle of tragedy to be broken or the system to change. American narratives of justice in the 1930s vacillate between the image of the extraordinary Everyman of Mr. Smith or Mr. Deeds saving democracy, and the doom of Eddie and Joan losing their lives to the system.

The power of Hollywood images was palpable and, to some, upsetting. While films were extremely popular with audiences, conservative politicians and clergy felt that the depictions of sexuality and crime here posed a threat to public morality. In the early 1930s, under threat of government intervention, the industry established internal censorship guidelines, known as the Hays Code (after Will H. Hays, who helped draft it) or more formally as the Motion Picture Production Code, which were enforced by 1934. Along with banning profanity, blasphemy, and depictions of rape, prostitution, "perverted" sexual acts, and specific crimes, the code also forbade "sympathy for criminals" and insisted that crime always be punished.

This was a response to the crime films of the early 1930s. The Production Code and the men behind it were not interested in examining what caused crime, why violence occurred, why women were raped, or why people acted in certain ways sexually, but only in banning their depictions. As important, the connection between sexuality and crime became embedded in the censors' and the public's imagination. The Production Code would be in place until 1968.

Impoverished Americans in these years thought about justice in complicated ways. Crime was on the rise, lynchings of African Americans occurred on a weekly basis, J. Edgar Hoover and the FBI began targeting men labeled sexual psychopaths (often code for homosexual), workers and leftists were often victims of police and federal government violence, and America was becoming a land of clearly defined outsiders, who were sometimes sympathetically portrayed in films. From the 1920s to the 1940s, movies, within a highly racialized context that ignored issues of gender and sexuality, portrayed American ideas of justice as questions of "Who counts as an American?" and "How can this system of democracy work with such economic disparities?" The idea of hate revolved around the construction of an idealized American identity. This view escalated as America entered a war against the clearly defined, and (in America's eyes) racialized, nations of Germany and Japan. The circumstances of who is hated and by whom are protean. Definitions of hate are never constant; they shift, focus, and refocus in relationship to events. During war, racial hatred looks like patriotism.

WAR: DEFENDING DEMOCRACY AND PATRIOTIC HATE

Hollywood fully engaged with the war effort and began producing films against the Third Reich before 1941. Anatole Litvak's *Confessions of a Nazi Spy* (1939) and Chaplin's *The Great Dictator* (1940) were harsh attacks on fascism. Propaganda for the Allied cause, these films promoted American democracy by demonizing the German national type and the Japanese with extreme racial stereotyping. The creation of the at-war Other was easy. The stereotype of the ruthless, barbaric Japanese drew upon orientalist images securely located in the American imagination.[5] The treacherous German Aryan was, on the surface, dangerously close to the idealized white, patriotic American Everyman. The difference that screenwriters seized upon to demonize German citizens was that they were *too* white, *too* similar to one another, and *too* patriotic in their willingness to blindly follow orders. They were, in a sense, the nightmare version of the average American.

All war films—home-front domestic dramas, USO musicals, romantic comedies of servicemen on leave, spy thrillers—bolstered a strong national identity and a united front against a common enemy. This is evident in men-at-war battle films such as Leslie Goodwin's *Parachute Battalion* (1941) or Lewis Seiler's *Guadalcanal Diary* (1943), in which average American servicemen bond together to fight fascism. Individual goodness in films of the 1930s was now transformed into a collective good. To counter the homogeneity of the stereotypical German military, Hollywood films emphasized a multiethnic American military of soldiers of diverse classes. Here the Anglo, Irish, Italian, Jewish, Protestant, Catholic, college-educated, working-class, and sometimes even the "Negro" bonded to fight for American democracy. These films presented simple narratives with often contradictory messages in which individual bravery is only valued in a collective context, nationalism is a pathway to peace, diversity is valued to distinguish it from fascism, and justice and goodness are achieved—and demonstrated—through the violence of war.

These contradictions are embodied in Mervyn LeRoy's *The House I Live In* (1945), an eleven-minute fictional short written by Albert Maltz that features Frank Sinatra singing "The House I Live In," which praises American democracy and racial tolerance. The narration is built around Sinatra confronting a pack of preteen boys in an alleyway who are harassing a neighborhood boy because he is a Jew. Sinatra calls them a pack of "Nazi werewolves" and explains that America is made up of "a hundred different kinds of people, and a hundred different ways of talking, and a hundred different ways of going to church, but they're all American ways." He then tells them about two American flyers, a

Presbyterian and a Jew, working together to bomb a "Jap battleship." Problematic as it is, *The House I Live In* was a precursor of postwar films that began to overtly examine race hatred and prejudice in America. Films such as Elia Kazan's *Gentleman's Agreement* (1947) and Edward Dmytryk's *Crossfire* (1947) exposed American anti-Semitism. Richard Brooks's *Home of the Brave* (1949) and Kazan's *Pinky* (1949) took on anti-black racism. These films labeled prejudice "anti-American," and like the war films were an ode to American bravery in fighting "foreign ideas," specifically race hatred, but on the home front. Even as they avoided larger questions of institutionalized racism or collective responsibility, the films began a more in-depth public discussion of religious and racial prejudice.

The strong, if flawed, ideal of social fairness in many of these films was countered by a diametrically opposed sensibility in film noir. The clear message in Tay Garnett's *The Postman Always Rings Twice* (1944) and Billy Wilder's *Double Indemnity* (1944) was that the modern world was filled with fear, isolation, betrayal, and a lack of human connection, only intermittently redeemed by love. Low-budget films delivered this message with a more existentially bleak view. Mark Robson's *The Seventh Victim* (1943) and Edgar J. Ulmer's *Detour* (1945) presented an America in which justice and fairness were absent and ultimately irrelevant.

As the war brought many Americans together, it also exposed the desperation of the human condition and the difficulty, if not impossibility, of finding justice. Despite the optimism of the postwar era, and advances made in some social justice movements, there was a growing pessimism in American culture that negated the ideal of a cohesive society founded on a collective identity. Noir films posited a combative nihilism that set people against one another, often for power or money, basically because humans could never be entirely decent or fully good.

■ ■ ■

Despite America's triumph in the war and booming economy, the post-war years were characterized by disillusionment and a growing realization that the American ideal had not been, or could not be, achieved. This was compounded by the tremendous fear of losing the new cold war and the anxiety that the new prosperity could cease. Ideas about hate, justice, and goodness both solidified and mutated in the films of the 1950s.

COLD WAR JUSTICE

The ideologies of the Cold War produced a clear non-American Other who was a distinct and deadly threat to an idealized America. In the decade's film and television, this othering is best understood in the omnipresent shadow of the deaths of the Holocaust and Hiroshima, as well as in the fear of new technologies and science. The postwar context was filled with dangerous others whose shapes and forms kept morphing until they became indistinguishable and interchangeable. They took the form of invading intergalactic creatures from distant planets who threatened human life on earth, prehistoric or atomically mutated monsters who came from beneath the sea or deep caves, international spies (often from Communist countries) who threatened US security and peace, and even American citizens who threatened the American way of life. Sometimes this last group was rebellious teenagers who fractured the American family, or political extremists at either end of the spectrum who threatened the democratic process. Some 1950s films used the outsider to critique a broken social system.

The invader is the most obvious of these manifestations, most often present in science fiction and horror films aimed at a teen audience. The alien invader, often suggesting communism, is central to science fiction films such as Howard Hawks's *The Thing from Another World*

(1951) and William Cameron Menzies's *Invaders from Mars* (1953). Alien threats were not limited to the body politic, but to the human body as well. Don Siegel's *Invasion of the Body Snatchers* (1956) and Louis Vittes's *I Married a Monster from Outer Space* (1958) are nightmares of physical intrusion and psychological annihilation. Some films did not view the alien as hostile. Films such as Ib Melchior's *The Angry Red Planet* (1959) and Robert Wise's *The Day the Earth Stood Still* (1951) used aliens to critique and warn human civilization to be less destructive—especially in its use of atomic energy. Nightmares of social and physical disorder were connected to radioactivity from the atomic bomb. Gordon Douglas's *Them* (1954), among numerous other films, featured insects becoming monstrous and deadly.

Masculinity, central to American identity in the 1950s, was always under attack. Society was seized by enormous cultural anxiety that the male body or mind could be compromised through invasion by aliens or the misuse of science. The message in Jack Arnold's *The Incredible Shrinking Man* (1957) and Herbert L. Strock's *I Was a Teenage Frankenstein* (1958), both films about the misuse of science, is clear: American manhood is under attack. The connection between traditional, idealized masculinity and an American political ideal is highlighted by the enormous popularity of the comic book hero Superman, who, according to the television show *The Adventures of Superman* (1952–1958), was dedicated to "truth, justice, and the American way."

Despite its obsession with the threat of the outsider, 1950s film and media culture was nuanced. Ideas about justice and fairness, innocence and guilt were actively debated in numerous Hollywood films. One example is Sidney Lumet's *12 Angry Men* (1957), which took on issues of racism and class inequality. These critically acclaimed and popular films drew upon themes similar to those in the science fiction movies, but countered fear-mongering with pleas for understanding the outsider.

In much the same way, while teenagers were portrayed as dangerous delinquents in Jack Arnold's *High School Confidential* (1958), they were also frequently portrayed—as in Laslo Benedek's *The Wild Ones* (1953) or Nicholas Ray's *Rebel Without a Cause* (1955)—as outsiders who challenged adult culture.

This more nuanced approach is evident in many Westerns. Frequently containing explicit and casual racism toward Native peoples, and always told from a white perspective, these films were often reflections on America's history of violence against Native peoples, but used these narratives to comment on contemporary issues of racial identity and discrimination. Films such as Delmer Daves's *Broken Arrow* (1950) and John Ford's *The Searchers* (1956) dealt with issues of racial identity, interracial relationships, and the legal status and oppression of Native peoples in complex ways. Clear connections were sometimes drawn between the treatments of Native peoples and African Americans.

The Western was used to explore other contemporary issues. Fred Zinnemann's *High Noon* (1952) and George Stevens's *Shane* (1953) grappled with serious questions of pacifism and how violence affects the rule of law. Television dramas such as *Gunsmoke* (1955–1975), *Have Gun—Will Travel* (1957–1963), and *Bonanza* (1959–1973) used Western settings to discuss contemporary questions of racial equality and interracial friendships. The Production Code prohibited explicit violence, so much of the gunplay in these film Westerns was tame, often offscreen. This lack of explicit violence also reflected these films' critique of violence or of using it as anything other than a last resort. Television Westerns contained even less violence, for similar reasons. Despite its title, the central character in *Have Gun—Will Travel* rarely used a gun and was committed to solving problems through discussion and not violence.

Despite the emphasis on invasion, and social and bodily violations that were all understood to be rationales for hating, the media of the 1950s provided a vital public forum for ideas about fairness. Discussion was rooted in the social justice themes of 1930s films, the democratic ideals that emerged during the war, and the momentum that activist movements gained in the postwar years.

The golden age of television was a product of postwar prosperity that promoted an engaged civil discourse about justice. This was an outcome of the influence of writers and producers who came of age in the more politically radical 1930s. Shows such as *The Philco Television Playhouse* and *Playhouse 90* featured live dramas, almost always from a liberal perspective, about crime, racism, juvenile delinquency, drug use, alcoholism, medical ethics, and marital infidelity. These bold political narratives carefully individuated issues of responsibility for both good and bad acts. There was little critique of the judicial system or economic inequality—responsibility for unethical acts lay with individuals.

These forthright attempts to deal with social and ethical issues were complemented by women's films and television. Mark Robson's *Peyton Place* (1957) and Douglas Sirk's *Imitation of Life* (1959) explored themes of responsibility and ethical behavior in relationships and domestic settings. Dealing with large issues such as the role of women in the workplace, sexual double standards, and the politics of motherhood, their soap opera narratives prevented them from looking at a broader context. When they did suggest that there were larger issues at stake, such as race in *Imitation of Life*, they often timidly avoided their own presumptions by resorting to sentimental appeals to an emotional status quo. Many films of the 1950s were concerned with questions of equality and the place of the outsider in American society. As the postwar civil rights movements were making legal gains and establishing popular support, there was a vital synergy between affairs of state and movies that was new to American culture.

GLIMMERS OF GOODNESS

Social changes in the 1960s and 1970s were quickly reflected in Hollywood films. World War II and the Cold War fundamentally defined US politics and culture from the late 1940s through the 1960s. This began to change in the 1960s. The very visible 1963 March on Washington drew attention to and reenergized the black civil rights movement. Also in 1963, the publication of Betty Friedan's *The Feminine Mystique* ignited the second wave of the women's movement. Both reshaped national political discourse. At the same time, the very-much-alive Cold War was now focused on Vietnam as a proxy for Soviet Russia, and colonial rule in Asia and Africa began to crumble because of national liberation movements, although its effects still were often catastrophic for governments as well as individuals in numerous countries. The National Liberation Fronts in Algeria and then Vietnam made national political struggles part of a global discussion. By the late 1960s the more radical ideologies of black liberation and women's liberation substantially reshaped the goals and the strategies of preexisting, more moderate, movements.

National and world politics were being discussed in broader contexts and with the sense that all political struggles were connected. Simultaneously, there was an increasingly accepted understanding that "the personal is political." This new consciousness, building on the thinking of Freud, Wilhelm Reich, R. D. Laing, and Herbert Marcuse, among others, proposed a more complex understanding of the relationship between the individual and global politics. This thinking influenced the counterculture, sexual liberation, the antiwar movement, feminism, black power, and gay liberation, and increased the tension between the politics of individualism and a collective, even global politics.

Hollywood films and television of the early 1960s reflected the liberal ideas of the later 1950s media. John Frankenheimer's *The Birdman of Alcatraz* (1962) and Sidney Lumet's *The Pawnbroker* (1964) explicitly dealt with issues of class, the legal system, and anti-Semitism. A new wave of weekly TV dramas reflected a similar politics. Police, lawyer, and hospital dramas such as *Naked City* (1958–1963), *The Defenders* (1961–1965), and *Dr. Kildare* (1961–1966) grappled with ethical and moral issues. Even *The Twilight Zone* (1959–1964) consistently posed questions of justice and outsiderness. These shows were a reflection of contemporary social justice movements, seen through a post–World War II lens as well as the antiestablishment sentiments of 1930s film. They reflected a reformist mindset that presumed a basic goodness in human behavior and were culturally in sync with the Civil Rights and Voting Rights Acts, as well as with other social welfare programs such as Medicare/Medicaid, food stamps, and Head Start.

This liberal trend ended in the mid-to-late 1960s with the rise of the Hollywood independent film and the advent of a vibrant youth counterculture closely tied to the antiwar movement. The independent films, produced and directed by artists in revolt against the studio system, manifested clear political ideologies. Arthur Penn's *Bonnie and Clyde* (1967) was a meditation on America's culture of violence; Dennis Hopper's *Easy Rider* (1969) was an analysis of traditional American masculinity; and Robert Altman's *M*A*S*H* (1972) offered a devastating critique of the Vietnam War. These films grappled with ideas of personal responsibility and the place of American power in the world. In this they reflected the growing antiwar sentiment in the United States, and an increased awareness of the consequences of violence and social injustice. They rejected the liberal sentiments of films of the later 1950s and through the mid-1960s that had presented a more utopian, all-you-need-is-love vision and the belief that violence was not only controllable but possibly even eradicable.

The rise of the independent film, as well as the change of public attitudes about sexual behavior and drug use, finally brought about the demise of the Production Code. Hollywood films now portrayed more sophisticated ideas about sexuality, criminal behavior, and everyday American life. Legal ideas about sexual representation also changed. In 1969 the Supreme Court relaxed the nation's censorship laws, at first allowing people to more easily purchase sexually explicit material. The legality of live and filmed theatrical presentations was left up to states and cities.

There was some public outcry about this new permissiveness. After a year of study, President Lyndon Johnson's Commission on Obscenity and Pornography stated that viewing sexually explicit material had not been proven to be harmful. In 1972 Bryanston Pictures, a small distribution company, released *Deep Throat*, a pornographic film centered on heterosexual fellatio. *Deep Throat* quickly became a focus of battle in the national culture wars over sexual expression. During the next four years state and local municipalities attempted, often successfully, to ban the film. The federal government entered this battle with a prolonged campaign supporting a ban, claiming that the film violated laws prohibiting the transportation of pornography across state lines.

In 1984 President Ronald Reagan asked Attorney General Edwin Meese to do another study. A year later the Attorney General's Commission on Pornography, known as the Meese Report, concluded that pornography was, to varying degrees, personally and socially harmful, and that the pornography industry had ties to organized crime.

Heavily criticized by the media, the Meese Report was taken up by some feminists who used it to argue that all pornography is intrinsically harmful to women. Women were defined, by this argument, only in terms of victimization. Activist Catherine McKinnon described heterosexual pornography as hate speech. Feminists actively debated porn throughout the 1980s; many feminists argued that heterosexual pornography constituted de facto violence against women, or caused violence against women. Much like the Production Code in the 1930s, the Meese Report, while eager to demonize and ban pornography, was not interested in understanding the causes of violence against women or in dealing with them.

The politics of this counterculture were often contradictory. The ideal of "all you need is love" was countered by the more nihilistic worldview of "sympathy for the devil." Embracing disorder, idealizing revenge, and extolling individualism, it sometimes saw violence as cathartic, and even a moral good. This sensibility harkened back to the pessimism of film noir, but with more overt violence. Alfred Hitchcock's *Psycho* (1960) is an early example. With their casual sadism and flippant attitudes about world power and politics, the early films in the James Bond series, such as Terence Young's *Dr. No* (1962), were harbingers of a major trend in filmmaking in a wide variety of genres.

THE COMPLICATIONS OF VIOLENT JUSTICE

Sergio Leone's *The Good, the Bad, and the Ugly* (1967) and Sam Peckinpah's *The Wild Bunch* (1969) recast US history not as dramas of violence between marginalized and dominant groups but as parables of anger and greed. Don Siegel's *Dirty Harry* (1971) and Michael Winner's *Death Wish* (1972) were urban thrillers that preyed on audiences' fear of crime and fueled the fantasy—in much the way *The Birth of a Nation* had—of justice through vigilantism. Some films used violence as a response to social changes. John G. Avildsen's *Rocky* (1976), about a white working-class amateur boxer triumphing over a popular black boxer, was developed and filmed during the early litigation of the noted *Regents of the University of California v. Bakke* Supreme Court case that challenged and overturned aspects of California's affirmative action law. Richard Brooks's *Looking for Mr. Goodbar* (1977), a cautionary tale of promiscuous sex, was a response to women's sexual freedom in the first decade of second-wave feminism. Francis Ford Coppola's *The Godfather* (1971) was an exception since it honestly portrayed characters dealing with issues of personal responsibility in the larger context of family, violence, and ideas about honor and justice.

The ideology of justice through revenge is entrenched across political ideologies in American culture. It is present in traditional genres produced by the studio system as well as renegade independent films. Alejandro Jodorowsky's surrealist Western *El Topo* (1970) is a counterculture version of *The Good, the Bad, and the Ugly*. Connections between revenge and justice are predominant in the blaxploitation genre in films such as Gordon Parks's *Shaft* (1971) and Jack Hill's *Coffy* (1973). Here African American revenge is used to fight racial injustice, but the underlying themes of celebratory violence leading to justice are similar to those of the James Bond series. John Shaft is, in essence, the urban African American Bond complete with a valorized hypersexual, masculine affect; in a series of films including *Coffy* and *Foxy Brown* (1974), Pam Grier's characters glorify the image of a hardworking, beautiful, and hypersexualized woman drawn to acts of revenge because no other realistic routes to justice are open.

The most pressing political issue of the late 1960s and early 1970s was the Vietnam War. With few exceptions, Hollywood's response to the issue only happened after the war ended in 1975, by which time public sentiment was decisively against it. This is in direct contrast to the numerous films produced about and during World War II and the Korean War. Television news during the Vietnam War was vigilant in its war coverage, and often critical of US policy. When Hollywood films did finally address the war, they were overwhelmingly against US intervention. Films such as Hal Ashby's *Coming Home* (1978), Ted Kotcheff's *First Blood* (1982) and its sequel *Rambo: First Blood Part II* (1985), and Oliver Stone's *Born on the Fourth of July* (1989) presented a range of approaches. Some films focused on the lives of soldiers and their families and grappled with an individual's making of moral decisions. Other films such as *Rambo* explicitly critiqued the US government, foreign policy, and military leadership, although not addressing larger geopolitical causes or the national moral ramifications of the war. Much of the focus and approach, as in *Mr. Smith Goes to Washington*, highlighted the individual's story, not the larger social or political context.

In the post–Vietnam War films, antiwar sentiments were not necessarily based on pacifism, especially when it came to the enactment of justice. The extraordinarily popular slasher film genre that emerged alongside the antiwar films is a prime example. Horror films "brought the war home," moving its violence into the world of the American teenager. These films glorified the brutal killings of attractive young women and men by revenge-seeking psychopaths, often linking the deaths to sexual activity. Beginning with John Carpenter's *Halloween* (1978; seven sequels), Sean S. Cunningham's *Friday the 13th* (1980; eleven sequels), and Wes Craven's *Nightmare on Elm Street* (1984; eight sequels), dozens of similar films were released. The genre fused the apprehensions about war with anxieties over a cultural embrace of more open sexuality.

Because the teen victims lack individuality, the movies fundamentally valorize the psychotic outcast seeking violent revenge for an imagined or real slight. The vigilantism in *The Birth of a Nation* is simple compared to what is happening here. Jason, Michael Myers, and Freddie (in *Friday the 13th*, *Halloween*, and *Nightmare on Elm Street*, respectively) become valorized antiheroes for a post–Vietnam War culture. They are American soldiers killing innocent victims (who, the films imply, are not all that innocent), and they are also psychotic killers who need to be stopped, even as it is clear they will always return. The messages here are conflicted. Is the return of the killer the return of a vanquished hate? Are the killers actually misunderstood and misguided moralists? While the films glamorize, even justify, their vigilantism, they also reassert traditional, if temporary (and usually police-enforced) order at the film's end. One of the Vietnam War's legacies in American culture is that it profoundly scrambled ideas of whom it was possible to hate, what justice might mean, and what goodness could look like.

The revenge, slasher, and blaxploitation genre films of the later 1970s signaled the emergence of a cultural ideology that was antithetical to the liberal, coalition-based political critiques of the previous years. Revenge films portrayed vigilantes as morally right, if functioning in a world of amorality. Slasher films portrayed them as psychotic, if historically and psychologically inevitable—Freddie Krueger is a perfect example of the return of the repressed. Blaxploitation films portrayed them as heroic, arguing that vigilantism was the only sure way for African Americans to find justice. Each of the genres advocated and justified vigilantism as an exciting and workable form of justice.

Traditional revenge films were unconcerned with the social order—the world was intrinsically chaotic and human beings were amoral. Slasher films restored a social order, with the understanding that, inevitably, it would be violated again. Blaxploitation films envisioned a new, less racist, social order of equality. While each of these genres promoted very different ideas about social and legal control, they were produced during, and influenced by, an era when "law and order" sentiments were taking hold on the American popular, and legislative, imagination.

In 1968 Chicago mayor Richard Daley ordered city police to attack antiwar protesters during the Democratic National Convention. New drug laws, passed when New York governor Nelson Rockefeller decided to get tough on crime before a presidential bid in 1974, meted out harsher penalties for drug convictions that led to the rise of mandatory sentencing laws. Rockefeller's tough-on-crime reputation was based on his reaction to a prisoner takeover in protesting to mistreatment and appalling living conditions at Attica Correctional Facility in Attica, New York. When negotiations for the release of hostages broke down, Rockefeller sent in state police, and in the violence that ensued, forty-four people, including ten correctional officers and civilian employees, were killed.

In 1976 the Supreme Court reasserted that capital punishment was constitutional four years after the court had essentially declared a moratorium on it. The resurgence of support for the death penalty was emblematic of the popular acceptance of retaliatory killing as a form of justice, not unlike the ideas portrayed in Westerns, but now enacted under the social form of law and order. This tough-on-crime thinking resulted in a major expansion of the US prison system. From 1980 through the 1990s, prison construction escalated while the state and federal prison population mushroomed from 500,000 to almost 1.4 million. Many more people were also incarcerated in city and county jails, immigrant and juvenile detention centers, and territorial, Indian Country, and US military facilities.[6] In 1993 the emergence of the "three strikes you're out" laws in many states reinforced the idea that a crackdown on crime would make a safer United States. These policies substantially ensured that the US criminal legal system would intensify its retributive focus.

The "get tough" theme, with the emergence of a different paradigm of justice, is evident in television's presentation of legal and policing issues. Television dramas in the 1960s, such as *The Defenders*, focused on defending criminals and on how the law, while well intentioned, did not serve justice and needed to be transformed. By the later 1970s and early 1980s, the tone and political messages were changing. *Starsky and Hutch* (1975–1979) presented hip undercover police who were so close that some viewers saw homoerotic implications in their relationship. The show supported the existing criminal legal system—they still caught bad guys and put them in jail—but the tone was light. This was a kinder, gentler, more personalized police state.

Charlie's Angels (1976–1981) featured three beautiful women with James Bond–like skills and presumed a good guy/bad guy dichotomy, but the "Angels" were essentially private detectives and the show's focus was on light entertainment. *Hill Street Blues* (1981–1987) humanized the police, and to a lesser degree the criminals, but began constructing an urban world in which crime was rampant and justice increasingly harsh. By 1990 a series of television police shows, most notably with the twenty-year run of *Law and Order*, began to radically change representations of law enforcement. Police procedurals have increasingly become a television network staple—by the 2013 fall season there were twenty-two of them—including *CSI: Crime Scene Investigation*, *Castle*, *NCIS*, and *The Mentalist*—all determinedly promoting law enforcement, prosecution, and imprisonment as the *only* route to justice.

Hollywood's portrayals of policing agents' ability to provide "law and order" were more ambiguous, avoiding television's simplistic good guy/bad guy vision. Jonathan Demme's hugely influential *Silence of the Lambs* (1991) featured Clarice Starling, an emotionally tortured FBI agent, pursuing—with the help of Hannibal Lecter, a serial-killing psychiatrist and cannibal—another serial killer who skins women. Riffing off themes from *Psycho* and the slasher movies, *Silence* ostensibly broke from older ways of thinking about justice, making Lecter a charming, even elegant foil for Clarice, who is haunted by dreams of failure. Scrambling expectations of criminals and law enforcement is not a new narrative technique. Film noir did it more effectively, and films such as *Bonnie and Clyde* did it with greater political intent. The ultimate effect of *Silence of the Lambs* is to render questions of guilt or innocence irrelevant rather than present them in a new light.

Popular action films such as John McTiernan's *Die Hard* (1988) and its sequels, Doug Liman's *The Bourne Identity* (2002) and its sequels, and psychological thrillers such as Clint Eastwood's *Mystic River* (2003) or even a humorous film such as Stephen Soderbergh's *Ocean's Eleven* (2000), replicated some of these ideas, often ironically. The *Die Hard* series' antihero is a social and romantic loser who has to redeem himself and his manhood; Jason Bourne is an amnesiac in search of his identity; and the men in *Ocean's Eleven* are all nice guys with larcenous tastes. These more nuanced characters and plots reflected changing attitudes about how complicated morality and justice might be.

The same is true of the new wave of superhero films featuring Batman, Spiderman, Superman, Green Lantern, and others, which gained increasing popularity during these years. Using cartoonish images and plots, they presented audiences with surprisingly sophisticated ideas of right and wrong, justice, and goodness. The superhero genre is based on myth narratives that portray universal truths complicated by human fragility and morality. Like contemporary action films, their appeal rests in their moral ambiguity about justice.

Beginning in the 1990s, independent films such as Spike Lee's *Jungle Fever* (1991), John Singleton's *Boyz n the Hood* (1991), and Callie Khouri's *Thelma and Louise* (1991) offered more intricate ideas about personal responsibility and violence. These new political visions did not, however, create a more vibrant cultural discussion.

Cable television has emerged as an important entertainment venue in the past two decades. Because it is not subject to the regulatory constraints of network television, cable has the potential to approach difficult material with emotional maturity and political nuance. HBO's *Oz* (1997–2002), for example, viscerally exposed the grueling details of prison life, though its basic message—good guys versus bad guys—was different from that of earlier shows only in that roles were switched: some prison guards were now bad guys and some prisoners were good guys. This formula was present in an organized crime setting in HBO's *The Sopranos* (1999–2007). The series never glamorized members of the crime family as it humanized them; however, neither did the show give audiences the larger perspective on moral structure found in *The Godfather*.

Breaking Bad (AMC, 2008–2013) and *Dexter* (Showtime, 2006–2013) feature bad guys who do terrible things but were presented as antiheroes. *Breaking Bad's* Walter White, dying of cancer, embarks on a two-year crime spree of drug dealing and violence to ensure his family's financial well-being. As his crimes increase in ferocity, he becomes more heroic, if not more understandable, especially after he dies while wiping out a group of neo-Nazis. Dexter Morgan, an analyst for the Miami Police Department, is a secret serial killer who metes out his own lethal justice to criminals who have avoided legal justice. As in *Silence of the Lambs*, we are invited to relish a psychopathic killer less as an antihero than as a perversely righteous hero. Many of these newer shows have broken from the most traditional rhetorics of good and bad, right and wrong, legal and illegal by viewing them through a skeptical lens. This, however, is less a critique of the original moral or ethical terms than it is a parodical approach that, in the end, reinforces these terms.

MYTHOLOGIZING HATE

Representations of hate and justice in American film and media are contradictory. At times some of these images promote violence, social misunderstanding, race or class antagonism, and hateful attitudes, but they cannot be reduced to only this. They constitute a popular cultural history of how actual people understood, and grappled with, their own hate and the social conditions under which they lived. Film and television affect how we think, but our individual and group reactions to these images also shape the world around us and, consequently, promote the creation of new images. The poverty and social disarray of the 1930s influenced the crime dramas of the time—and the films themselves reaffirmed people's sense of justice, pain, and disenfranchisement.

Over time and through technological advances, these interactions have compounded. Since the 1930s, news sources have proliferated, television has brought the world into our living rooms, Hollywood studios have become involved in multiple media and marketing ventures, and multinational media corporations have eventually come to dominate the market. We now experience more media images than ever before. The messages they disseminate vary widely and wildly—there is no single accepted and agreed-upon articulation about hate and justice.

Connections between myths about hate in the dominant culture and the history of representing hate and justice in films may appear tenuous. There are so many representations that it would be easy to find an example and an exception for any argument. Looking at the historical scope of ideas about hatred and goodness that films have offered American audiences, it is clear that these myths, as well as public policy, do not emerge from one decade, one political moment, or one motion picture.

They are the product of decades of social, legal, and political evolution. Specific politics may change, along with whom we value as citizens, but hate will always be impossible to completely pin down and contain. Hate-based violence erupts, and often more violence—physical, emotional, verbal—is then used in an attempt to eradicate violence. The power of film is that it can move us with the stories of characters who are facing complicated decisions. We learn from these stories about what hate, justice, and goodness may mean to us and to our society. What we frequently do not learn from these films, however, is how our individual emotions are part of, and responses to, a far larger social and political fabric of which we, and our communities, are a part.

3

BOUNDARIES, BORDERS, AND PSYCHIC SHADOWS OF HATE

"I imagine one of the reasons people cling to their
hates so stubbornly is because they sense, once hate is gone,
they will be forced to deal with pain."

—JAMES BALDWIN, "Notes of a Native Son"

Many people conceptualize hate as primarily a personal emotion, assuming an individual's hateful, perhaps violent, speech or action emerges from a deeply internal enmity. Even when people discuss it as a group phenomenon, say, in a lynch mob, they imagine the group as made up of hate-filled individuals for whom the group functions as a support system. But individual and group expressions of hatred are largely given shape and organization through larger social structures. Society's cultural fixation on hate borders on an obsession, influencing cultural norms and shaping legal and policy decisions. Society rarely examines the community-based effects or the social costs of their current preoccupations with evil and enmity.

The Reverend Martin Luther King Jr. noted that the war in Vietnam "is but a symptom of a far deeper malady within the American spirit." One form this malady takes is our fascination with hate. It is

relatively easy to chart the expressions that hate takes and the immediate damage it does. More difficult is to explicate how this obsession
works in everyday psychic, cultural, and political life. Understanding
the origins of these feelings may allow us to face them more directly.
The concept of "the abject" is useful here. In her book *The Powers of
Horror: An Essay on Abjection*, Julia Kristeva describes the abject as an
idea, object, or person that rejects or disturbs accepted thinking, or the
communal consensus that underpins a social order.[1] This is best epit-
omized by the images of the rotting corpse as that which was once human and is now not human, and therefore a horror, since it reminds us
of our corporeality and limited power as mortals. The abject is not just
the rotting corpse but any thing, person, or group that, for symbolic or
imagined reasons, disgusts us, or makes us uncomfortable in our own
bodies because it is not us.

This idea illuminates how the psychic development of a group or
individual can be formed not by what they stand for but by what they
fear or despise. (It is possible, though, to mistake one for the other by
recasting one's disgust as proof of goodness.) Kristeva's concept makes
even more sense when considered in conjunction with Simone Weil's
idea of force as being "that which turns a person into a thing."[2] Weil's
notion of force here can be as extreme as the act of killing, but also
can refer to denying a person or group basic rights and access to such
necessities as food, housing, education, health care, and employment,
thus depriving them of aspects of their humanity. This kind of force,
while not outright murder, is nonetheless an expression of the ethic of
supremacy and inferiority. It takes longer, but exerted over time, it also
deprives people of psychological, spiritual, and physical life.

Hate is not simply an emotion. It is an element of relationship,
acknowledged or not, that exists in the physical world, affecting how
people live and how they relate to themselves and one another. It

destroys possibilities for the creation of vibrant and just communities, in which residents are bound together across differences by a compassionate sense of interdependence. These kinds of communities offer residents not only a sense of place, but also the goodness of belonging, not on the basis of conformity to dominant cultural mandates, but with individuation.

In her 1952 *The Need for Roots* Simone Weil argues:

> To be rooted is perhaps the most important and least recognized need of the human soul, and it is one of the hardest to define. A human being has roots by virtue of his real, active, and natural participation in the life of a community, which perceives in living shape certain particular treasures of the past and certain particular expectations for the future. . . . Every human being needs to have multiple roots. It is necessary for him to draw well-nigh the whole of his moral, intellectual, and spiritual life by way of the environment of which he forms a natural part.[3]

The hate frame prohibits giving priority attention to building and nurturing this sense of community and honoring those roots.

AN EPIDEMIOLOGY OF HATE

Hate is not a stable entity. It is volatile, taking numerous forms and appearing in different guises. All human emotion and endeavor is shaped by historical, cultural, and personal experience. To grasp the material and psychic ways in which hate manifests itself and to understand its consequences, it is useful to rudimentarily chart the basics of who is hated, by whom, and why.

How is hate schematized in our society? What people and what groups are liable to be hated? What are the historical and cultural conditions that surround this?

The most conspicuous category of people targeted for hate in the United States today are those seen as dangerous outsiders. This amorphous group carries numerous labels: criminal, terrorist, predator, pervert, disease-carrier, and extremist. This is strikingly evident in the antiterrorist rhetoric of American politics after 9/11 and in the images and narratives that animate anti-immigration campaigns. A nearly identical pattern is seen with people who are perceived by the majority as holding extremist political views. Left-leaning groups are particularly likely to be characterized as dangerous, possibly criminal, extremists. In the 1960s and early 1970s, the US Federal Bureau of Investigation's (FBI) Cointelpro (Counter-Intelligence Program) initiative, charged with discrediting and disrupting movements for social change, almost exclusively targeted advocates of social and economic justice and peace. High on FBI director J. Edgar Hoover's list were what the bureau characterized as advocates of "Black Hate," a Cointelpro category focused on the Reverend Martin Luther King Jr. and the Southern Christian Leadership Conference, the Student Nonviolent Coordinating Committee (SNCC), and other civil rights and black power organizations.[4] The political counter-response to liberation movements was to "get tough on crime." More recently, intense early media ridicule of the nonconfrontational Occupy movement, which emerged in 2011, sought to undermine its focus on rapidly increasing US disparities in distribution of wealth and income.

The same labeling dynamic applies to far right–leaning groups, although the labeling is inconsistent and those doing the labeling tend to be different. Law enforcement agencies historically have viewed advocates for progressive social and economic justice as intrinsically dangerous and subversive, even as the authorities have often ignored or even perpetrated violence directed against people of color and other marginalized groups. Law enforcement has, in rare cases, turned its attention to armed white supremacist and antigovernment survivalist and paramilitary groups. In 2009, under intense pressure by conservative media, the US Department of Homeland Security withdrew a report issued earlier to law enforcement agencies warning of the possible rise of right-wing extremism in the United States.[5]

In the public imagination, criminals, and criminal communities, are primarily pathological, wicked individuals and groups who can be freely hated. The identification and pursuit of criminals shapes the structure of American society and constitutes a staple of mass media and entertainment. There is an obsessive focus, particularly in print and broadcast news, as well as on episodic television, on individuals who are suspected or have been convicted of breaking the law. The so-called reality series *COPS* aired on the Fox network from 1989 to 2013; when Fox canceled the series, Spike TV picked it up. A host of other shows built on the same premise have proliferated. The various series spun off from the show *Law and Order* have been fueled for over two decades by promoting fear of characters based on their criminal, or potential criminal, behavior. This is particularly true for people who are suspected of, charged with, or arrested for (though not necessarily convicted of) what is labeled predatory sexual behavior.

The case of Nushawn Williams is a prime example of how a person, accused with circumstantial or unsubstantiated evidence, is represented individually as a social pariah embodying multiple threats to the social order, and is used to fuel broader processes of stigmatization. In 1997 Williams, a twenty-year-old African American man from Jamestown, New York, was accused of purposefully transmitting HIV to female sexual partners. A crack dealer with a criminal record and a history of violence against women, Williams had unprotected sexual contact, after being told that he was HIV positive, with forty-seven women, two of them sexually active teens below the age of consent. Fourteen of these women were discovered to be infected with HIV, although it was unclear if Williams was the cause of these infections. (Two children of Williams's partners were born with HIV as well.) Posters with Williams's photo were placed around Jamestown, urging anyone who had had sexual contact with him to contact authorities.

When the Williams story broke, a national media frenzy ensued. Headlines like "When Children Fall Victim to AIDS Predator"[6] and "Two Births Lengthen List in One-Man H.I.V. Spree"[7] were common. The *New York Times*, whose coverage was relatively subdued, reported that Williams was "charged with a deadly swath of predatory sex." News reports across the country referred to Williams as a "one-man epidemic" and an "AIDS Monster." A year later the case became the basis for a *Law and Order: Special Victims Unit* episode.[8]

Williams's case raised a number of important concerns, including the possibility of quarantine for people presumed to be spreading a disease, the efficacy and ethical integrity of public health measures for tracking a disease, and the legal culpability of an HIV-positive individual having unprotected sex. Significantly, none of the adult females with whom he had unprotected sex were considered responsible for their consensual participation. All of these issues, and the possibility of discussing them responsibly, were overshadowed by the media frenzy that rushed to endorse flawed criminal "solutions."

As a poor black man with a drug habit and a criminal record, Williams was already placed outside of acceptable society. He was certainly acting unethically and irresponsibly by not informing his partners of his HIV status. His sexual partners also acted irresponsibly by failing to prevent transmission of the virus. As a sexually active person with HIV/AIDS, he was already technically a criminal in some jurisdictions. Thirty-seven states have laws mandating stiff sentences for intentional and unintentional transmission of HIV. Some of these laws even criminalize sexual activity for HIV-positive people if they engage in protected sexual behavior but do not disclose their HIV status.[9] The presumptive crime here is not the infliction of intentional or even unintentional harm but simply the status of being HIV positive.

The symbolic threat posed by this group (criminals, terrorists, predators, and extremists) is that they are considered inherently disorderly. Their very presence is not symbolic of danger; it *is* danger. They exist outside of the accepted social order and perceived moral boundaries of society. In Western culture the concept of existing outside the accepted social order is rooted in theology. Both the Hebrew Bible and Christian scripture make clear that God has a plan for the world and human behavior. To stray from that, to commit sin, is a social as well as a moral transgression. From the fifteenth to the seventeenth centuries in Europe, there was little distinction between sin, as defined by canon law, and what we now consider criminal behavior. After the rise of the nation-state, countries began to codify their own legal codes, such as English common law, and these were based, largely, on canon law. This is particularly evident in laws that criminalize various forms of sexual behavior such as sodomy, fornication, and adultery. Christian theology was also at the root of laws demonizing racial difference to justify slavery, condemn race-mixing, and prohibit interracial marriage.

These theological origins are obscured because contemporary secularized society has little understanding of its religious underpinnings. Our language, however, often betrays these origins. The word *evil*, for example, is historically a theological term. Augustine claimed that evil was not a thing, but simply the refusal to do good, that is, refusal to act morally.[10] Since World War II, the term has been used with increasing frequency in describing trends in global politics as well as human behavior. Hitler, the Holocaust, and Nazism have been routinely called "evil." Fascism itself has not necessarily been considered evil; Generalissimo

Franco in Spain escaped the common use of the label, no doubt because the Vatican, as well as the US government and American business interests, supported him. Hannah Arendt famously described Adolf Eichmann as embodying "the banality of evil." Ronald Reagan described the Soviet Union as "the evil empire" in 1983, and in his 2002 State of the Union address, George W. Bush described Iran, Iraq, and North Korea as "the axis of evil" for their alleged accumulation of weapons of mass destruction as part of a global campaign of terrorism.[11]

High-profile criminals such as Jeffrey Dahmer (who between 1978 and 1991 sexually assaulted and possibly cannibalized sixteen young men), Ariel Castro (who between 2002 and 2004 kidnapped three young women and held them, for a decade, as sexual hostages in his Cleveland, Ohio, home), and James Eagan Holmes (who killed twelve people and injured seventy in an Aurora, Colorado, movie theater shooting in 2012) were routinely described by the media as "evil" and "monsters." Their crimes were dreadful; they generate a visceral response. The use of the word *evil* here is purposeful and selective. By reserving this word for selectively publicized acts, we shape the conversation to exclude acts that are not as obviously horrific.

The word *evil* is never commonly used to describe state-sanctioned violence such as the United States' involvement in the assassination of Chilean president Salvador Allende in Chile and its support of the murderous military junta that followed. Theological language, divorced from its religious underpinnings, is used only when it is politically convenient.

The second group of people made easy targets for hate are those perceived to be outside accepted religious, gender, political, class, or race norms. The common denominator here is that all of these identities are noncriminal; they are targeted for animus simply because they fall outside a social or cultural norm.

Dominant culture assumes that all those labeled criminals, terrorists, predators, and extremists are hated because of perceived actions. But there is considerable overlap with those who are targeted because of their identity. (Sometimes identity alone is enough for society to ascribe presumptive criminality.) Individuals who fall outside prescribed gender norms, for example, are at high risk for discrimination, poverty, and violence. A 2011 National Center for Transgender Equality and National Gay and Lesbian Task Force study showed that 19 percent of transpeople had experienced intimate partner violence at the hands of a family member because of gender nonconformity. Less surprising and more prevalent, 78 percent of transpeople had experienced harassment in an educational environment; 31 percent of transpeople had been harassed by teachers or staff. In that same context, 35 percent experienced physical assault, 5 percent by teachers or staff. Significantly, 29 percent of all transpeople and gender-nonconforming people have reported being harassed or treated disrespectfully by police officers.[12] Reports from the National Coalition of Anti-Violence Programs confirm that transgender people of color are especially likely to be singled out for abuse and violence, including murder.

It is easy to believe that groups that are now more powerful were never targeted for hatred. The history of Roman Catholicism in the United States is replete with examples of intolerance, discrimination, and violence. In two days of rioting in 1834, an Ursuline convent in Charlestown, Massachusetts, was burned by a mob of Protestant anti-Catholic agitators. A decade later, in May and July of 1844, American nativist groups in Philadelphia fomented riots that torched and used cannons to attack two Catholic churches, a convent, a rectory, and Catholic-owned homes. Scores were injured and more than fifteen people died. Ostensibly the riots were a reaction to a Catholic school director's allegedly banning Bible reading in public schools; the riots are called the Philadelphia Prayer Riots or the Bible Riots. The true causes, however, were anxieties focused on jobs being lost to the increased numbers of Irish immigrants, the perception that Catholics could not be real Americans because they were more loyal to the Pope than to this country, and a host of fears that connected Catholics, particularly priests, to predatory sexual practices.[13]

Similar antialien sentiments are evident in numerous attacks on American mosques (or, in one case, a Sikh temple mistakenly thought to be Muslim) that have occurred since 9/11. The justifications for these attacks may be based on inaccurate or distorted beliefs about Muslim religious practices, suspicions of loyalty to foreign governments, and unease about perceived gender and sexual differences.

Violent attacks on people and institutions on the basis of actual or imagined religious and cultural differences are so woven into the fabric of US history that they often appear logical and transitional—a sort of national hazing process; a ritual that leads to American tolerance and acceptance of diversity. In this way America's bold, often successful, ongoing struggle to accept some cultural difference cloaks the harsher reality of structural violence.

The third group of people targeted for hate consists of individuals, and sometimes communities, who allegedly elicit disgust because of their physical appearance, presumed proclivity to spread disease, or deviation from sexual or gender norms. Overlaps exist with the previous groups, but the impetus to hate people in this group arises from the virulent response of disgust by people who consider themselves to be ordinary arbiters of acceptability.

Parameters here are nebulous; the boundaries of who is, or what about them is, hated are variable. Why are some disabled people socially upsetting and some not? The young woman with an amputated leg in a wheelchair elicits pity, while the child with autism who cannot speak or stand still makes onlookers profoundly uncomfortable, but the Gulf War veteran with a severe facial disfigurement arouses deep feelings of revulsion. This response illuminates Kristeva's abject: we find horrific that which we associate with the less-than-human, and which we fear we could become. This is articulated succinctly by a character in Fred Zinnemann's 1950 film *The Men*, about paraplegic soldiers returning from World War II. In a hospital group discussion about how they will reenter society, Norm (Jack Webb) spits out, "Face it, we will never be accepted. We remind them too much of who they might become."

Disgust as a response to disability or illness has long-standing roots in Western culture. Church teaching in the Middle Ages suggested, although it did not officially declare, that leprosy, then untreatable, was a punishment for sexual sins. Cities passed laws forbidding lepers from living there and forcing them, as they approached others, to ring a bell and declare themselves "unclean." St. Gregory of Nazianzen argued that lepers were barely human and were "men already dead except to sin."[14]

These actions were eerily replicated in the early years of the HIV/AIDS epidemic as people with AIDS, many of them stigmatized gay men, were evicted from their apartments, fired from their jobs, denied medical treatment, and viewed as unhuman monsters being punished for their sins. Today we do not officially ban disabled people from the public sphere. Rather, the fear of people who are disabled is expressed as pity, a dismissive form of sympathy that places them in a dependent category of not-us. The question is not one of rights, which is a civic requirement, but of charity, which is inconsistent and dependent upon private generosity.

Some sexual acts are considered disgusting when performed by certain people but not so when performed by others. The social construction of disgust is evident in the widespread heterosexual revulsion of gay male anal sexual activity. This disgust is so accepted that it even emerges in public debates about the legality of same-sex marriage. Yet many heterosexuals engage in similar activity. Some studies show that up to 56 percent of heterosexuals engage in anal sex.[15] It is a staple of heterosexual male pornographic fantasies. This is also true, although with less revulsion, with heterosexual reaction to homosexual acts of oral sex. In *From Disgust to Humanity: Sexual Orientation and Constitutional Law*, legal scholar Martha Nussbaum deftly demonstrates how culturally bound ideas of disgust are profoundly influential in shaping American law.[16] Disgust for lesbian and gay people remains strong enough to fuel political debates about the legal status of homosexual activity and even same-sex marriage. Nussbaum posits a simple progression—from disgust to humanity—that is heartening and essentially progressive, but potentially misleading. Visceral emotions such as disgust do not disappear so much as morph and resurface under new guises, ideologies, and actions; not despite the fact, but because they are shaped by social and cultural forces.

What society calls hate is a set of responses to an interwoven set of historical, cultural, and physical stimuli and circumstances. With such myriad, confusing manifestations, hate has become a catchall word, easily manipulated for political ends. By pausing before labeling an action or emotion as hate, people may be able to create a space in which they can make clearer, more careful judgments about the collective and individual consequences of emotions, language, and actions emerging from animus.

Everyone is implicated in various ways of causing harm. The hate frame allows people to distance themselves from such behavior. Simone Weil argues that, "A hurtful act is the transference to others of the degradation which we bear in ourselves. That is why we are inclined to commit such acts as a way of deliverance."[17] Until people understand these feelings and psychic states of mind and how they function in the political world, society will never be able to take full responsibility for them.

INEXTRICABLE CONNECTIONS BETWEEN FEAR AND HATRED

Understanding how everyone is implicated in hate, and the harm it causes, is challenging. The idea that hurtful acts are a way of cleansing ourselves of internal damage and projecting that damage onto others is closely connected to people's relationship with fear.

Connections between fear and hate are, on a superficial level, obvious. Fear instills a dread of some person, action, or object; an immediate, self-protective response is to hate what is causing that fear. Experiments have documented that most humans are revolted by bodily excretions—pus, vomit, urine, excrement, nasal discharge, menstrual blood, saliva—because, like Kristeva's rotting corpse, they are reminders of human mortality. Symbolically, they blur the boundaries of being alive and being dead; of being human and being an object. Psychologist Paul Rozin calls these "primary objects of disgust." (Blood when inside the body is not considered disgusting, but when outside the body it is. Tears, however, are the exception because we assume, inaccurately, that humans are the only animal that sheds them, and so they have become a symbol of our humanity.)[18]

The fear of death is omnipresent in people's lives, and Kristeva argues it can be best understood in the fear instilled by horror literature and film. From John William Polidori's novella *The Vampyre* (1819) through the classic Hollywood horror films such as Tod Browning's *Dracula* (1931), haunting/possession films such as *The Omen* (1976), and slasher films such as *Halloween* (1978), to supernatural/psychological thrillers such as *The Ring* (2002), based on the popular Japanese film

Ringu (1998) audiences have long craved horror and the fear it induces. Despite the terrifying nature of abjection horror films, which portray drinking blood or stitching together dismembered corpses, remain extremely popular.

These films function as a safety net that allows us our fears in a safe environment. As the classic advertising quote originated by horror director William Castle for his 1964 thriller *Strait-Jacket* advised, "Just keep telling yourself, it's only a movie." There is a more complex reason for the attraction to horror and fear. Fear has a dual nature: it frightens, but there is also pleasure, even a seduction in the fright. Fear is a response to a real or imagined danger that gives us a physical jolt of excitement.

The stimulus for the so-called fight-or-flight response could be a spider, a knife at one's throat, a crowded auditorium, the waiting for an anxious person to speak, or the sudden thud of one's front door against the door frame.[19]

This excitement and heightened physical reaction to it is similar to the sexual excitement of stimulation, arousal, climax, and resolution. We want to experience it again and again. With horror films the pleasure of the fright is contained; we know it is only a movie. Fear in the material world—of being assaulted or robbed, or losing control of one's car—is not contained, and therefore not pleasurable. This fear may be useful and allow us to adjust our behavior to avoid danger. But it may cause people to react in ways that are hateful and harmful to themselves and others. When George Zimmerman shot and killed Trayvon Martin he may well have experienced fear, as he claimed, but this fear may have been a reaction to Martin being an African American man, and Zimmerman's response was excessive and deadly.

In thinking about the relationship between fear and hate, Herbert Marcuse's distinction between "necessary repression" and "surplus repression" may be useful.[20] By analogy, "necessary fear" arises in situations that may cause people physical harm such as running from a fire or an explosion. Surplus fear, on the other hand, is the same reaction to a situation or a person that is not intrinsically harmful, but that people have been socially conditioned to fear. An example of surplus fear would be believing that a person with HIV/AIDS is an imminent danger to one's physical well-being. Another, classic example of this kind of fear—a paranoiac fantasy—is the 1960s urban legend that hippies were spiking suburban water supplies with LSD.

These fears are predicated on what Nussbaum calls "projective disgust": disgust and fear that "can hardly bear rational scrutiny."[21] The media enshrine these culturally constructed fears in our everyday social consciousness. Here they become very real fears and shape laws, public policy, and the ways we respond to one another. Media frenzies inflame needless public fears over a wide range of issues, including rising crime rates, drug usage, teenage pregnancies, murderous children, road rage, and mutating viruses. These public panics are fueled by two primary factors.

The first is an increasingly manipulative media, which, for the sake of ratings, promote fear in every aspect of our personal and social life. This promotion of fear that we know, on some level, will not affect us personally carries the thrill of the horror film. Alfred Hitchcock famously stated, "There is no terror in the bang, only in the anticipation of it," and the power of this alarmist media is that they suggest something catastrophic (and unlikely) just around the corner.[22]

Public panics are also fueled by the fact that their fear confirms and sustains preexisting prejudices and social structures. In the fourteenth century, for example, impure water was an everyday problem. It was only when the anti-Semitic myth began to circulate that Jews were poisoning the wells of Christians (an earlier version of the hippies and LSD) that the issue became a major cultural preoccupation.[23] Fear, especially when carefully manufactured, can bolster existing animus against a group and convince others to be fearful. Fears are not random or matters of happenstance. They arise out of historical conditions, and a culture picks and chooses which fears it will allow.

Fear has a payoff. Hate, and the language and actions it engenders, is the end result of fear. It is the psychological bang of the bomb in the Hitchcock quote. There is also a social and political payoff. Manufactured fear reinforces social, cultural, and political norms, and hateful language and acts ensure, even with force, that those systems are kept in place. The very human pleasures of fear, whether in horror films, news reporting, or urban legends, implicate all of us in the process of fearing and then hating.

In December 2009, plans for an Islamic cultural center (first called Cordoba House, now known as Park51), to be built two blocks from the site of the 9/11 attacks, were announced. The center was to contain a mosque. Early media response was positive to neutral, but national controversy erupted after anti-Islamic bloggers organized a campaign opposing the center. Inaccurately branding the project the "Ground Zero mosque," they claimed it would be a victory monument for the perpetrators of 9/11. The Anti-Defamation League and politicians such as Sarah Palin, Mitt Romney, Rudy Giuliani, and Ed Koch came out in opposition to it. By August 2010 a CNN poll reported that two out of three Americans opposed the center. Few of these Americans hated Muslims or Islam. The politicians involved made these statements for political gain. Public hysteria, started by American anti-Islamic activists, was inflamed by inaccurate information presented in rational "point/counter-point" debates on CNN and Fox News featuring the usual talking heads declaiming the expected conservative and liberal political points.

The controversy over Park51 was about partisan politics, but opponents used Islam to ignite fear. Tension over religious difference has always played a key role in many American culture wars. The phrase "war on religion" figures prominently in contemporary political debates. Conservative news outlets such as Fox News, far-right websites such as the Liberty Institute, and far-right bloggers such as Michele Malkin routinely use it. The "war on religion"—by which they mean the "war on Christianity"; the attacks on Park51 were never described in the news as a "war on religion"—has become a ubiquitous reference to a wide range of policy and legal issues. The conservative complaint of a war on religion is not new. The 1962 Supreme Court ruling in *Engel v. Vitale*, which banned prayer in public schools, is cited as the beginning of clear tensions arising from the enactment of legal boundaries concerning religious belief in a secular society. Supreme Court decisions in 1984 and 1989 addressed issues about the placement of religious symbols, especially crosses and Christmas crèches, on public land. There have also been campaigns by secularists to remove the phrases "one nation under God" and "in God we trust" from the pledge of allegiance and US currency.

More recently, the "war on religion" has focused on the use of the conscience clause, which is said to allow believers full access to their First Amendment right of the free exercise of religion. A conscience clause is added to laws, policies, and professional contracts, allowing medical professionals such as doctors, nurses, and therapists to refuse to perform an act, such as an abortion or the distribution of contraceptives or safe-sex information, that violates their religious beliefs. Conscience clauses originated in 1973 after *Roe v. Wade* legalized abortion, but have since been applied to clergy who do not want to perform same-sex marriages and, most recently, Christian-owned commercial establishments such as bed and breakfasts that refuse to facilitate same-sex wedding events. Tensions have always existed over the relationship between law and religious beliefs in a secular society. The rhetoric of a war on religion inflames and distorts complicated legal issues and creates a climate of fear: "Christianity is under attack!" Religion is a pretext here, cloaking the core issues of politics, power, and difference.

Slavoj Zizek compares two very different visions of political engagement. The first, which we live with today, "resorts to fear as its mobilizing principle: fear of immigrants, fear of crime, fear of godless sexual depravity, fear of the excessive state itself, with its endless burdens of high taxation, fear of ecological catastrophe, fear of harassment."[24] Fear is the central mobilizing political principle in the United States today. This fear is often manufactured and fanned by politicians, the media, and commercial interests who benefit, economically or through the accumulation of power, from pitting people against one another.

The second vision of political engagement that Zizek discusses is a "radical emancipatory" politics "based on a set of universal axioms," which seeks commonalities between and among people and sees them as neighbors with a shared humanity. Here he references the epigram, "An enemy is someone whose story you have not heard."[25] Zizek notes the radicalism of Mary Shelley's *Frankenstein*, in which, after he has been voiceless, the monster is allowed to tell his story. In a shocking reversal of Simone Weil's definition of force, "that which turns a person into a thing," the now-reanimated parts of dead bodies become the means by which a person tells his story. Creation, biological and aesthetic, gives internal life to what was previously only a "thing."

The double-sidedness of fear is revealing here. As thrilling as it is to be frightened (the monster is terrifying in the first part of the novel), it is more thrilling to be relieved of that fear when the monster becomes a person. After the novel's 1818 publication, the name Frankenstein was transferred, in the popular imagination, from Doctor

Victor Frankenstein to his monster. The distance between human and monster, between person and object, is frequently portrayed as impossible to traverse. Yet it is negotiable because that divide is located within ourselves. The potential for identification and commonality is always there.

Media-produced fear is intentional and fosters a culture that inhibits people's ability to reflect upon difficult and nuanced ideas. It reduces issues, and questions that underlie them, to simple binaries of good/bad, either/or, left/right, black/white. These emotionally thrilling, fear-based narratives are commodified as entertainment. Advocacy organizations on the right and left, as well as religious and political groups, often promote a similar way of thinking that allows anyone who disagrees with their positions to be dismissed as an enemy.

ENDLESS WAR

The presumption that justice, and, even goodness, can be obtained through force is completely congruent with the bellicose language of war frequently used to describe human interactions and mobilize constituencies for political campaigns and even social justice work. War occupies a huge place in the Western imagination. It is enshrined in myths, folktales, and literature. It is understood to be the inevitable, logical conclusion to personal and national disagreements. The myth of war is that it wins back honor and power. It has been the impulse behind much of US policy throughout its history. In the public imagination, and popular culture, the horrors of war are almost always offset by its honor and its integrity.

The militarized metaphor of war has been used for centuries. The idea of a war between good and evil is a staple of theological and religious writing. When someone is pulled in two directions, she is said to be at war with herself. Notably, "the war between the sexes" is commonly used to describe gender relationships. War metaphors are ubiquitous in our daily speech: battlefield, join the ranks, war zone, no man's land, crossfire, blockade, bombshell, foxhole, hold down the fort. War imagery even brings the hint of violence to sex when Jean Harlow and Marilyn Monroe are referred to as blonde bombshells. Since the 1950s, war metaphors have become a staple of US public policy. They are easily adapted to both scholarly and popular writing about criminology, where urban areas are called "war zones," law enforcement agents are on the "front lines," and police "launch" a new initiative to curtail crime. Our language is a language of war.

Lyndon Johnson introduced "the war on poverty" in his 1964 State of the Union address as part of his plan for the Great Society. In 1971 Richard Nixon signed the National Cancer Act and declared a war on cancer. Later that year Nixon called for a war on drugs. This was an early stage of Nixon's "tough on crime" policies. These policies, a public relations move, were popular because of media panics surrounding the "lawlessness" of antiwar protests, the counterculture, drug use, and changing sexual mores. In 2011 George W. Bush declared a war on terror.

In the media, the language of war is used by conservatives and liberals. The October 26, 1998, issue of *Time* described Matthew Shepard's death as part of a "War Over Gays." *Rolling Stone*'s March 18, 1999, issue featured "The Holy War on Gays." The *New York Times* ran an editorial on July 27, 2013, titled "Mr. Putin's War on Gays." In 2011 Robert Reich, former secretary of the treasury and liberal commentator, began using the phrase "the war on workers' rights," which was taken up by the Teamsters as an organizing slogan at the end of 2013. In the 2012 election Democratic leaders Nancy Pelosi and Barbara Boxer, focusing on Republican resistance to reproductive rights, accused Republicans of waging a "war on women." The phrase quickly became headline material in print and television media, and its use increased in August 2012, when Todd Akin, US representative from Missouri, stated that "legitimate rape" rarely led to pregnancy. Used by the Left or the Right, the war metaphor oversimplifies the complexity of each of these problems, which are rooted in social, political, and economic conditions. The use of threats and the promotion of a climate of fear never address these realities, but actually are used to avoid addressing them.

Rhetorical similarities aside, there are distinct concrete consequences to these uses of "war." Language is never just a means of communication. It embodies and articulates a society's worldview. It circumscribes how we think about problems and challenges, and what we do about them. All of these situations call for changes in government policy. Efforts aimed at dealing with measurable threats to people suggest solutions that mobilize and expand existing social systems. The war on poverty called for federally funded education and food assistance programs; the war on cancer sought greater funding of the National Institutes of Health. Campaigns that are predicated on threats from people such as criminals and drug users always suggest solutions that include increased domestic policing and imprisonment. The endless pursuit of enemies internationally, including the amped-up US war on terror, continually escalates reliance on increased militarization, deployment of armed forces, and support of military and paramilitary units in other countries. Domestically and internationally, the United States has institutionalized torture. A prime example of this is the use of solitary confinement, which, as administered in the United States, meets international criteria for torture. Solitary confinement is routinely used in US prisons, and has been widely condemned. Even local police forces are now heavily militarized in what has become a "permanent war" society.[26]

This second group of war campaigns has led to escalating reliance on local, state, and federal levels of policing and incarceration to address a wide range of entrenched social problems. Since the 1970s these initiatives have steadily expanded. Harsher sentences—including, in particular, for drug-use convictions, mandatory minimums, as well as the growth of the private, for-profit prison industry—have driven mass incarceration. According to the Sentencing Project, the United States leads the world in incarceration, with at least 2.2 million people behind bars in 2012—"a 500% increase over the past thirty years" that far outpaced growth in violent crime rates. The number of women in prison has increased at nearly double the rate for men.[27]

UNCOMFORTABLE CONTAINMENT

Federal, state, and local criminal legal measures do not successfully address the social and economic conditions that produce violence. Conservatives look for the roots of violence in theological or medical/pathologizing explanations. The idea that a lack of personal responsibility causes violence is embedded in Christian thinking. Here violence and crime are the result of an individual moral failure: a sin. Or they are caused by a psychological disturbance such as sociopathy or psychopathy. Concepts of sin and spiritual failure have historically been linked to mental illness. In 1670 British theologian Richard Baxter argued in *The Signs and Causes of Melancholy* that mental illness, what he called melancholy, was caused by "loving self and the world too much: and the secret Root or Cause of all this, is the worst Part of the Sin, which is too much Love to the Body and this World."

Liberals argue that socioeconomic factors such as poverty are responsible for creating environments that produce violence. However, they rarely critique the role of larger structures such as capitalism, free markets, and the class system in creating poverty. The liberal analysis is hampered by the idea of individual solutions, not collective efforts. The crime films of the 1930s such as *Dead End* locate the cause of crime in the culture of poverty, but the problem is usually fixed by a renegade district attorney who takes on the legal system or a crusading social worker who inspires street youth to make better choices. The conservative and liberal positions are mirror images. Both conservatives and liberals focus on the individual. Conservatives blame crime on the individual who is unable to make the correct moral choices. Liberals turn to the individual to make moral choices to solve the problem. Neither analysis is sufficient or has the insight of Helder Camara, archbishop of Olinda and Recife, Brazil, who served during the repressive military dictatorship from the 1960s to the 1980s: "When I feed the hungry, they call me a saint. When I ask why people are hungry, they call me a Communist."[28]

Hate and crime-based violence emerge from the dynamic interrelationship of numerous, often structural, factors. Individuals clearly make personal decisions but frequently do so in the context of poverty, lack of access to adequate education, inadequate job protections, underemployment, lack of decent housing, and abusive policing. These factors do not force an individual to do any one thing, but they do help shape psychological makeup and expression, and they limit the material options available to people. The American impulse to personalize any problem is strong and persistent. The challenge of finding a balance within one's sense of individual moral responsibility—*not to act unethically*, or *to act ethically* and do good in the world—is not easy. Yet this challenge is hardly exclusive to impoverished people; it is germane to all of us.

The inability to deal with the larger social problems produced in significant measure by systems of human triage—processes by which persons and groups are ranked in terms of worthiness—and to grapple with questions of personal responsibility has intensified a national project to identify and isolate extremists and criminals. Historically this has defined itself along lines of race, class, ethnicity, and religion. Incarceration rates for people of color indicate that they are at much higher risk of arrest and imprisonment. More than 60 percent of people in the nation's jails are people of color, overrepresented relative both to their participation in crime and their percentage of the population. Black people constitute only a little more than 12 percent of the US population and Latino people comprise about 17 percent—together, just under 30 percent. In the early twenty-first century, black men have a 1 in 3 lifetime chance of being imprisoned; Latino men a 1 in 6 chance, and white men 1 in 17. For women, the disparities are even more extreme. Black women have a 1 in 18 chance, Latinas 1 in 45, and white women 1 in 111.[29]

Since the late 1990s, according to sociologist Nancy A. Heitzeg, a cluster of educational policies and practices have transformed US schools "from sites of opportunity and inclusion into centers of criminalization and exclusion."[30] The proliferation of zero-tolerance policies and an increased police presence in schools have criminalized even minor school disciplinary infractions. The result: a school-to-prison pipeline that removes students from educational settings through suspension, expulsion, or arrest, placing them on a track to juvenile and adult criminal legal systems. The forces driving mass incarceration drive the school-to-prison pipeline: fear of crime, belief that harsh sentences and exclusion from the community will produce safety, and selective enforcement/racial profiling. Students of color are much more likely to face harsher discipline: about 40 percent of students expelled annually are black; 70 percent of students involved in in-school arrests or referred to law enforcement are black or Latino; and black students are three and one-half times more likely to be suspended than whites.

■ ■ ■

The cultural significance of this is greater than specific rates of imprisonment and the extralegal harassment of particular groups. This historical and contemporary shaping of a national story runs wildly counter to the traditional American narrative of ever-increasing inclusion. America has provided opportunities for many people and groups. This has not always been the case in the past, and it is not always the case now. From the persecution, imprisonment, and occasional execution of religious dissenters such as Quakers and Catholics in the earliest American colonies, to the confinement and genocide of Native peoples, to the intense antiblack violence rooted in chattel slavery that continues to shape race-neutral social and economic policy, the historically persistent psychic shadows of animus are ingrained in our national story.

FAILED ANALYSIS/FAILED SOLUTIONS

It is easy to see the maladies of spirit affecting the United States today, all of them profoundly affected by individual hatreds and structural forms of violence. Rights and recognition are not evenly distributed; neither are multiple forms of violence. Poverty is created not by the individual failings of morally compromised people, but by the decisions of the powerful and wealthy. American society seems incapable of taking this evidence seriously. Many civic and religious leaders simply don't want to. The result is a system in which many people, if only in small ways, enjoy social and economic benefits that come at the expense of others. These benefits emanate from the very structures that reflect ever-morphing versions of the same maladies that have haunted American society from its earliest beginnings: the ethic of exclusion and expendability, and the ideology of supremacy and domination.

Laws and policies, by their very nature, often cannot get to the root of the problem because people seem hesitant at best, and afraid at worst, to address the real issue. Society's tendency is to tinker only with symptoms. Beginning in 1995 a series of class-action lawsuits filed by inmates in California state prisons charged that overcrowding prevented the basic mental health and medical needs of prisoners from being met. In 2005 Federal District Court judge Thelton E. Henderson placed the prison health-care system in federal receivership. In 2009 a three-judge panel ordered the state to cap its prison population at 137.5 percent of capacity. To conform to constitutional standards, California was ordered to release forty-three thousand inmates within two years.[31]

What looked like reform produced little real change. Ignoring prisoners' rights groups who were lobbying to reduce prison populations by making fundamental changes in sentencing laws, Governor Jerry Brown instead signed contracts with several for-profit corrections companies. These included the Corrections Corporation of America, which had contributed to his campaign and supported several of his administration's initiatives.[32] In January 2014, California officials announced they expected a growth of ten thousand inmates in the state's prison population over the next five years. Almost all of these inmates will go to for-profit prisons.[33]

Critically necessary reforms, such as confronting the unconstitutional lack of medical treatment in prisons, are needed. But they cannot change the core issues of criminalization of communities of color, poor people, and people with mental illnesses. Laws and policy are put in place to benefit existing power structures.

Many people would like politicians to solve these problems, even when society needs better, more honest and effective, politicians than are now in office. To view the problem simply as one for institutional politics misses the point. Everyone has, to varying degrees, an emotional investment in holding on to feelings of fear and hate. Most people use hate in some measure to shape their lives, to establish borders and parameters between them and others, between their identities and other identities. Human beings have strong impulses to destruction or harm. These occur even in the name of peace and community. The history of war demonstrates that. Even when faced with an obvious, avoidable tragedy people tend to rely on their old analyses and replay the scripts they have always used to feel safe.

When the public imagination is so shuttered, it becomes impossible for people—and societies—to do anything different from what they have already been doing. It becomes impossible even to think about alternatives.

People are unable to reconsider hate and move away from fear because, consciously or not, they do not want to confront the possibility of unwanted emotional and psychic changes in themselves. They are so intellectually and emotionally attached to the existing world that they cannot see the larger structures that facilitate fear and violence. To the extent that society cannot embark on new processes of reconsideration and reflection, it cannot create new cultural symbols and narratives for people to relate to one another and to the world. Society has been unable to create a new societal ethic and language for encouraging empathy and goodness as options in everyday life.

New ways of communicating such an ethic could lead to a shift in consciousness, helping people begin to think differently and envision new justice practices rooted in a shared recognition of humanity. Policy shifts alone will never produce the needed changes. Our society suffers from what Dr. Martin Luther King Jr. called maladies of the spirit.

MALADIES OF THE SPIRIT

Maladies of the spirit take numerous forms. They are not restricted to racism, crime, economic injustice, and bullying, but a broader set of spiritual disorders that prevent society from thinking coherently about justice and goodness in ways that dismantle beliefs and structures rooted in an ethic of domination. One malady upon which many other disorders rest is a lack of trust. The roots of fear and hatred are located in the absence of trust: trust in others, trust in our communities, trust in ourselves, and trust in our ability to do good. And why should we trust, given this nation's history?

A beginning might be in radically breaking from society's preoccupation with evil and enemies. It would be necessary to replace this language with an expanded civic vocabulary of goodness. This new vocabulary could develop as new social structures of public goodness are being created. The challenge is not to invent new words but to select different ones and expand ways in which the goals of justice practices are envisioned and communicated.

This might take the form of helping people financially without enacting the old forms of dependent and pitiable charity. It might mean finding new ways of conceptualizing race that would honor difference and not stigmatize it. It could mean holding people and institutions accountable for their harmful actions in ways that strengthen community well-being.

The challenge is to think very differently about the nature of justice itself; to imagine accountability beyond the confines of punishment; to think about justice as a means of expressing compassion; to reclaim lives rather than dismiss them; to establish strong and just social, cultural, and economic relationships rather than strive for retribution; to openly seek to dismantle structural forms of violence; and to create peaceful and sustainable communities without relying on an unjust and violent criminal legal system.

Working at the intersection of multiple forms of violence, organizations such as INCITE! (radical feminists of color working to end violence against women, gender nonconforming, and trans people of color), Creative Interventions (promoting community-based responses to interpersonal violence), Generation Five (working to eradicate child sexual abuse), Project NIA (working to eradicate youth incarceration), and Seattle's Communities Against Rape and Abuse have been engaged with such questions for many years. The resources that they and other organizations offer can help to ignite our imaginations and to change our language of justice from one of hate to one of public goodness. The first step is to begin to trust that whoever our neighbor is, he or she is not automatically a threat to us.

4

COLLECTIVE RESPONSIBILITY
AND MORAL DISENGAGEMENT

"A mob always begins inside us; never is it an outside job.
Always it is an inside job: the troublemakers are there,
but they are inside you and me."

—LILLIAN SMITH

In 1923, Rosewood, a small, predominantly black, economically prosperous community on Florida's northern Gulf coast, was burned to
the ground during a week-long race riot instigated by white people.
Local and state authorities did little to stop it. At least two white residents and at least six, perhaps as many as seventeen, African Americans
were killed, although many more were injured or had their homes destroyed. The community's black population fled during the violence;
none returned.

The history of Rosewood's race riot was lost until 1982, when a Florida newspaper wrote about it. A television special followed, as did John
Singleton's feature film *Rosewood* in 1997. In 2004 a cast-aluminum
Florida Heritage roadside marker memorializing Rosewood was placed
at the site, a full decade after state approval of a $2.1 million apology
allocation. The last known survivor of the Rosewood riot died in 2012.

The story of Rosewood, like much racist violence, is depicted as an irrational episode of racism that erupted and then disappeared. This narrative is false. The violence in Rosewood was the logical outcome of social conditions and historical circumstances. A revival of the Ku Klux Klan in 1915 profoundly shaped racial attitudes during the 1920s. Violence, intimidation, and threats against African Americans created a culture of silence regarding black experience. Much of the violence directed at Rosewood was a deliberately considered attack on African American economic independence. Whites resented black prosperity, which undermined white economic dominance. The violence in Rosewood was not about fear of difference, but a sustained set of actions for economic gain.

At the center of the Rosewood story are questions about responsibility: Who bears responsibility, and what kinds of responsibility, for addressing massive harm? Who is responsible for dismantling the policies and practices that produce it?

The most common response to these questions entails people proclaiming "not me," quickly followed by public displays of outrage, always directed against others. Most people refuse to engage with these questions in any substantive moral way. Zizek notes that "our ethical responses remain conditioned by age-old instinctual reactions of sympathy to suffering and pain that is witnessed directly."[1] This is why an act of violence that receives sensationalized media coverage is, to many, more horrible than other forms of violence that harm, even kill, a thousand nameless people. When people acknowledge the existence of mass violence, they seldom grapple with the question of responsibility, which is often wrongly reduced to a question of legal culpability. In a culture that articulates a sharp division between good guys and bad guys, where almost everyone identifies as the former, this makes perfect sense. The hate frame allows people to morally disengage from considering how they are implicated in harming others.

Many people, confronted with evidence of massive harm, sympathize at first and then, seeking emotional distance, back away. They want to avoid the pain as well as separate themselves from the weight of responsibility. They often sincerely want *someone* to deal with it, but the more widespread the pain, the more they turn away. People select proxies to act for them rather than engage morally or politically themselves. The primary proxy is the criminal legal system, itself a perpetrator of systemic violence.

From 1972 to 1991, members of the Chicago Police Department, led by commander Jon Burge, coerced confessions from at least 119 suspects and witnesses by subjecting them to numerous methods of torture.[2] These included beatings, genital torture, electric shock, choking, dry submarino (near asphyxiation with a plastic bag), death threats, burning, mock executions, and denial of food, water, and use of toilet facilities. All of those who were tortured were African Americans, among them a thirteen-year-old boy. Officers administering the torture frequently used racial slurs.

An investigation by the Department's Internal Affairs unit confirmed systematic abuse, but special prosecutors declined to pursue the matter. Some of those convicted on the basis of false confessions—five from Illinois's death row—were imprisoned for more than two decades before being exonerated; one man was held for thirty-one years. Many others have been denied new criminal court hearings and remain in prison. The People's Law Office, representing victims of governmental misconduct, notes that two Chicago mayors, numerous police officials, and the Cook County State's Attorney's Office were implicated in the abuse and cover-up. After years of litigation, community advocacy, demonstrations, and findings from the United Nations Committee Against Torture, the US government investigated. In 2010 a federal jury convicted Burge—not for crimes of violence but for perjury and obstruction of justice. He was sentenced to four-and-one-half years in federal prison. The city agreed to significant financial settlements for a handful of the survivors; others, because the statute of limitations has expired, have been unable to negotiate settlements. Settlements, however, are no substitute for justice.

Burge, not the only public official implicated but the only one charged, became the scapegoat; larger problems of power and abuse remain unaddressed. The so-called investigations, inquiries, testimony, and hearings have not generated a sense of responsibility among the police participants or public officials. The so-called bad-apple argument insists that no one but Burge is culpable, despite evidence documenting widespread abuse by Chicago police.[3]

Blaming Burge alone, and minimizing the extent and nature of the harm done, reassures people that the violence is less pervasive than it actually is. Most people would like to live in communities that are safe, just, and compassionate. Exploring the best approaches to produce this safety, and ascertaining their impacts on those who are most affected by both systemic and bias-motivated violence is a difficult but necessary task.

Relying on the lens of hate doesn't work. It produces a too-limited analysis, and cannot diagnose multiple forms of violence borne by historically marginalized groups. The admirable goal of stopping hate does not produce new visions of justice or even raise questions about who is responsible for interrupting ongoing violence.

Systemic violence is always carried out in the name of the larger society, with public support and often with public resources; all members of society are in some way, intentionally or unintentionally, complicit in its continuation. Motives for tolerating injustice and violence arise from a combination of conscious and unconscious factors, and almost no one wants to accept the responsibility for them.

GUILT AND RESPONSIBILITY

Guilt is a major factor that discourages people from accepting responsibility for societal violence. Economic or political benefits play a part as well. Stung by the suggestion that they have done wrong, many people, as well as public and private institutions, rush to defend themselves: I did not personally torture anyone, or ask anyone else to do it. I have not physically abused a disabled person. Such deeply reactive thinking prevents more thoughtful reflection. It undercuts the opportunity for considering broader questions of ethics and responsibility. Most people and institutions respond to accusations or suggestions of responsibility with a counterattack. Accuser and accused become trapped in mutual recrimination, defense, and denial. Those with more political and economic power often win in the long run.

In 1945, considering issues of guilt and responsibility for the Holocaust, the political philosopher Hannah Arendt suggested that modern political concepts must accommodate new ways of thinking about culpability. "There are many," she wrote, "who share responsibility without any visible proof of guilt." In her opinion, those who shared broad responsibility for what happened included people who had supported Hitler in his rise to power and during World War II. "Who would dare to brand all these ladies and gentlemen of high society as war criminals? And as a matter of fact they really do not deserve such a title. . . . Yet these people, who were co-responsible for Hitler's crimes in a broader sense, did not incur any guilt in a stricter sense."[4]

Challanging the limited legal notions of guilt to illuminate more relevant questions of social responsibility, Arendt suggests that when governments bureaucratize degrading practices and violence, killing becomes an administrative feature of governance. In this situation a strictly political solution cannot suffice.

This insight is not limited to the horrors perpetrated by the Third Reich. The Holocaust is chillingly unique in form and scope, just as all genocides are unique and specific in nature. Societies establish moral benchmarks for what constitutes unacceptable mass dehumanization and violence. They vow that these abhorrent actions must never happen again. The hunt for identifiable criminals is intensified and the severity of punishments is increased in the belief that this eliminates the threat of recurrence.

This is an illusion. Angela Davis notes that racism is never a set of fixed strategies; it "changes and mutates over time. It does not remain the same while historical circumstances change." She argues that racism evolves and "hides" within social structures: "in the education system, the prison system, the health care system," and more, and thus "it can do more damage than ever without provoking the kind of resistance that led to the end of racial segregation."[5]

This constant morphing leads to lessened resistance when judgments about the wrongness of specific forms of violence are made in hindsight. Minor successes in fighting injustice often allow people to imagine that a particular form of violence will never happen again. In reality, the violence—or the group or the situation causing the violence—goes underground, reconfigures itself, and resurfaces. Old forms of violence are not recognized when they appear in a new guise because the illusory distance between "us" and "them" is reduced.

Distancing is an emotional and political strategy rooted in the belief of the superiority of some people and the inferiority of others. It justifies discrimination and exclusion. As Arendt maintains, it denies the possibility of a shared humanity and acceptance of responsibility for its well-being.[6] People and institutions refuse responsibility because it feels too great to bear. Yet deep, lasting change can only occur and be sustained by accepting responsibility.

A new understanding of common humanity must emerge. This phrase is often used to advocate for a blurring of real distinctions about how violence impacts various communities. The concept of colorblindness, for example, which ignores the very real differences in how people of various races are treated, allows the people with power to maintain it while denying that they are doing so. The sociologist Eduardo Bonilla-Silva characterizes this as "racism without racists."[7]

Colorblind logic establishes a national fiction that everyone is equal, even though most people don't believe it. The temptation for individuals to think of themselves, or their group, as superior to others, is compelling. The fiction of equality allows them to ignore the impacts of this on others and to disavow responsibility for producing structural inequalities and violence.

A LACK OF ETHICAL COHERENCE

By turning away from the impacts of violence on particular communities, and by refusing basic rights and recognition for some, individuals deny the humanity of others and themselves.

This simple observation provides a key to transformative change. American society recognizes and legitimates violence by ascribing it to "monsters." When many of the people said to be responsible for violence are known as good, decent people, there is a conceptual fracture: they are not the murderous criminals of the cultural imagination. Most people never recognize themselves among the ranks of those who are complicit in violence.

In his 1962 essay "Good People and Dirty Work," sociologist Everett C. Hughes notes mechanisms by which individuals and society keep "unpleasant or intolerable knowledge from consciousness."[8] This knowledge is easily accessible for anyone who cares to consider it. It is seldom acknowledged or openly discussed because to do so would be upsetting, and would threaten a group's or an individual's self-image and public reputation.

These mechanisms, found in families, organizations, small and large communities, and nations, include maintaining silence and justifying actions that violate the concept of common, or more precisely, shared, humanity. They keep in place group fictions that legitimate violence.

One such fiction reframes violence as normal, positive, and a pleasant way to build community. In the 1920s at least half a million American-born, Protestant, white women were active in the Ku Klux Klan. Many viewed their participation as an enjoyable form of friendship and relationship-building. An elderly woman from rural northern Indiana described this experience as "just a celebration . . . a way of growing up." Woven into everyday social life in myriad ways, white supremacist notions spread organically through neighborhood networks and family relationships. More recently, many women in contemporary white supremacist and neo-Nazi groups described having good relationships with mixed-race people and homosexual family members and friends, in contradiction with the group ideology to which they remained devoted.[9]

Physicians justified their involvement in Nazi programs of medical experimentation, euthanasia, and mass extermination by convincing themselves that these activities were necessary for the national and racial healing of the German people. Psychiatrist Robert Jay Lifton interviewed many of these physicians after the war. He wrote, "Neither brilliant nor stupid, neither inherently evil nor particularly ethically sensitive, they were by no means the demonic figures—sadistic, fanatic, lusting to kill—people have often thought them to be. . . . ordinary people can commit demonic acts."[10]

Almost half a million German women, nurses, office workers, social workers, and teachers who were implicated in mass murder in eastern Europe during World War II were not "marginal sociopaths." Ordinary people, often young and filled with a sense of national purpose, they believed their work was necessary to avenge their country against the enemies of the Third Reich.[11]

In Rwanda in 1994, an estimated 800,000 men, women, and children of Tutsi ethnicity were murdered and raped by members of the Hutu ethnic majority. Thousands of Hutus who opposed the slaughter were also killed. Anti-Tutsi grievances and antagonisms were stoked by national leaders, Radio Rwanda, and other media. Many ordinary people, including clergy, were complicit in facilitating, participating in, or failing to protest the killing of close neighbors. "What could I do?" asked a Catholic bishop who told a group of schoolchildren not to worry, that the police would protect them, even though, he had good reason to know, they would be killed.[12]

It is not necessary to be associated with the Nazis or some other "hate group" to be a good person implicated in dirty work. There are many people who work in institutional cultures that are permeated with violence. Even if most people oppose cruelty and abuse by correctional officials, they may not say anything when it occurs because to do so is to oppose the carefully constructed group fiction. If police and prisons are empowered to keep society safe, acknowledging that they themselves are perpetrators of violence is unthinkable. It is easier to believe that criminals deserve whatever they get because they are not part of the shared humanity. Law enforcement violence is framed as an inevitable, even essential, duty, as Everett C. Hughes observes:

> The minor prison guard, in boastful justification of some of his more questionable practices, says, in effect: "If those reformers and those big shots upstairs had to live with these birds as I do, they would soon change their fool notions about running a prison." . . . Furthermore he knows quite well that the wishes of his employers, the public, are by no means unmixed. They are quite as likely to be put upon him for being too nice as for being too harsh. . . . If, as sometimes happens, he is a man disposed to cruelty, there may be some justification in his feeling that he is only doing what others would like to do, if they but dared; and what they would do, if they were in his place.[13]

There are soldiers, conscripted and volunteer, who, finding themselves in the midst of war, live under conditions of constant stress, suffering the loss of comrades, and witnessing, or participating in, inhumane actions.[14] Others may not fit into any of these obvious categories, but nonetheless resist recognizing painful truths because it is just too uncomfortable.

Expiating culpability by violently displacing it onto somebody else is a theme in Charles Laughton's film *The Night of the Hunter* (1955). The story follows Preacher, a charismatic but ruthless confidence man who masquerades as a clergyman, while he is plotting to marry and murder lonely widows for their money. He charms others, in part, with his biblically inflected tale of how love vanquishes hate, illustrating the idea with the words *love* and *hate* tattooed on the knuckles of his hands. Preacher pursues Willa and a cache of money from a bank robbery stolen and hidden by her now-deceased husband.

Preacher is the quintessential confidence man. Gary Lindberg, in his study of the confidence man in American culture, notes that while society often defines confidence men simply as swindlers, they have a complex psychic appeal and infiltrate "the very centers of American values." Confidence men give voice to society's strongest aspirations and appeal to its deepest hopes; they literally "build confidence." These people have "infectious power" and are manipulators who create "an inner effect, an impression, an experience of confidence that surpasses the grounds for it. In short, a confidence man *makes belief*" even as his or her actions betray that belief.[15] Preacher metaphorically embodies many charismatic individuals who draw people close through false promises and the sheer force of personality. Willa's friends and neighbors, and ultimately Willa, are fooled.

Preacher murders Willa and pursues her runaway children, who now have the stolen money. He is stopped by the symbolic power of love, embodied in the character of Rachel, an elderly woman who is caring for the children. She turns him over to the authorities. Willa's neighbors form a lynch mob, their self-righteousness creating an impenetrable defense against acknowledgment of their earlier embrace of Preacher. Claiming to be an unambiguous force of goodness and justice, they seek to kill him to erase any evidence of their complicity in his violence.

Like Willa's neighbors, many people develop elaborate defenses to see only what they want to see in themselves and others. Attempts to justify or even deny the consequences of violence are part of a failed search for ethical coherence: society honestly decries violence and simultaneously perpetuates it on a massive scale.

There have always been people who refuse to remain silent. James Baldwin remarked to Margaret Mead in 1970, "I'm not interested very much in the question of guilt. What I'm trying to get at is the question of responsibility. I didn't drop the bomb. . . . And I never lynched anybody. Yet I am responsible not for what has happened but for what can happen."[16] Baldwin's straightforward embrace of responsibility is both unusual and refreshing.

COLLECTIVE RESPONSIBILITY

Mainstream American cultural and political thought mandates that force and violence be regarded in an individual context.

In 1986 the National Conference of Catholic Bishops issued a pastoral letter framing Catholic social teaching on the US economy as a commitment to economic justice for all.[17] Economic decisions have profound impacts on human dignity, the bishops claimed, and should be evaluated in light of it. "All members of society," they declared, "have a special obligation to the poor and vulnerable." In response, economist Milton Friedman, Nobel laureate and champion of unfettered markets, argued that because society is a collection of individuals, "only individuals can have moral obligations." In his view, a society, a government, or a country has no moral obligations to anyone. He decried the "collectivist moral strain" of the bishops' letter as "repellant."[18]

Together with his University of Chicago colleague Arnold Harberger, Friedman had served as academic mentor to a group of economics students from Chile. Known as Los Chicago Boys, the students returned to Chile, where they advocated Friedman's and Harberger's ideas, and were later asked by the Chilean military dictatorship of General Augusto Pinochet to restructure that country's economy. Pinochet seized power through a military coup that toppled the administration of the democratically elected socialist Salvador Allende. The United States knew of the coup in advance, and later, the US Central Intelligence Agency acknowledged its active support of Pinochet's regime.[19]

Los Chicago Boys implemented a number of free-market principles: dismantling labor unions, reducing wages, making draconian cuts in public employment, and privatizing public holdings and services. These policies ensured that ordinary people did not possess collective rights. The result was a highly efficient engine of upward redistribution, transferring public resources to private hands and encouraging the accumulation of wealth by a few at the expense of others. Broader public discussions of budget priorities never happened because the public sphere in which they should have occurred was functionally privatized.

Religious scholar William T. Cavanaugh believes these economic policies contributed directly to the overall climate of cruelty under Pinochet's regime. He suggests that the policies of Los Chicago Boys dovetailed with the systemic use of torture and the erosion of civil and human rights: both practices implemented the shattering of social bodies capable of collective resistance, such as political parties and labor unions, into isolated, compliant individuals through the infliction of fear and pain. The possibility of compassionate community was demolished by fear, betrayal, and silence. Cavanaugh maintains that anxiety is an effective tool for fracturing social bodies "because of its peculiar character as an essentially private phenomenon which nevertheless can be produced simultaneously in millions of persons within a given society."[20]

According to the Center for Justice and Accountability, during Pinochet's rule, "an estimated 2,600–3,400 Chilean citizens were executed or 'disappeared' while another 30,000 to 100,000 were tortured."[21] With covert US support, Operation Condor, involving secret police agencies of Chile, Argentina, Uruguay, Bolivia, Brazil, Peru, and Ecuador, sought to eliminate, through assassination and kidnapping, opposition to Pinochet's government in countries throughout the world.[22]

Cavanaugh argues that the clergy assumed at first that "the state was responsible for Chilean bodies, the church for Chilean souls. The church, in other words, had already handed the bodies of its members over to the state." When the state tortured those bodies, the church was unclear about its ecclesial responsibility. As things became worse, the church, in part, reimagined its collective relationship to the individuals being tortured and the torturers, the state, and even itself. The people of Chile must determine the effectiveness and integrity of that reimagining. It is significant that it happened at all. Under similar circumstances, around the world, other institutions have refused to engage in self-reflection.

People can stop violence by utilizing the lens of collective responsibility. In her 1945 essay "Organized Guilt and Universal Responsibility," Hannah Arendt argues that the concept of humanity, "when purged of all sentimentality, has the very serious consequence that in one form or another, men must assume responsibility for all crimes committed by men and that all nations share in the onus of evil committed by all others."[23]

Philosophical debates over the concept of collective responsibility have produced passionate responses and fierce fights over definitions.[24] Many conflicts are rooted in disagreement about whether corporations, communities, or governments can effectively be held accountable for massive violence. Friedman argued that institutions have no moral obligations; many others disagree. There are individual dilemmas as well. Accountability is an individual's obligation to answer for the consequences of her or his words and actions. Yet each individual in a system is not equally responsible for every harm that system produces. People who authorize, administer, or actively cover up harm are more directly accountable. There is, however, collective responsibility to acknowledge, interrupt, and, as much as possible, repair harm, as well as to work to change the conditions that produce it.

Anxiety and anger often arise in relation to the question of collective responsibility because politically, responsibility is linked to punishment. In a 2001 speech accepting a literary prize in Jerusalem, Susan

Sontag argued against the doctrine of collective responsibility as a rationale for the Israeli government's collective punishments against civilian populations in the West Bank and Gaza:

> I mean the use of disproportionate firepower against civilians, the demolition of their homes and destruction of their orchards and groves, the deprivation of their livelihood and their right to employment, schooling, medical services, untrammeled access to neighboring towns and communities . . . all as a punishment for hostile military activity that may or may not even be in the vicinity of these civilians.[25]

Many believe in collective responsibility *qua* punishment when "we" use it against "them," but not vice versa. Though collective punishment is prohibited by The Hague Regulations and the Third and Fourth Geneva Conventions, international law is difficult to enforce. Collective punishments are still utilized by many nations and political cohorts. Assessing decades of American denial of the moral cost of bombing Hiroshima and Nagasaki, justified in part as mass punishment, Robert Jay Lifton and Greg Mitchell write, "No country ever fully confronts its own history, least of all when morally vulnerable."[26]

Responsibility must be separated from punishment. To do so opens new understandings of collective moral engagement and agency rooted in an ethic of interdependence rather than of retribution. The idea of moral agency must be detached from the act of coercive moralizing, so that it can be envisioned as action that can interrupt the harm inherent in systems of domination and violence.

Rather than emphasizing guilt and blame, public focus might usefully shift to such concepts as societal accountability, healing, and redress. This might open new avenues for thinking about justice as right and compassionate relationship.

Chicago's Project NIA, a center dedicated to ending youth incarceration through the creation of community-focused alternatives to arrest, detention, and imprisonment, is one of a growing number of organizations engaged in such work. In Swahili, notes Mariame Kaba, the project director, NIA means "with purpose." The program is preparing communities that have been directly and adversely affected by mass incarceration to create effective strategies for change. This work challenges simplistic story lines about violence, victims, perpetrators, responsibility, and healing.

THE COMPLEXITY OF VICTIMIZATION

Narratives of victims and perpetrators are staples of popular culture. They inform American politics and produce a competition for victim status. Yet victims of violence and those who inflict it are not mutually exclusive categories. Angela Davis underscores this point: "the difficulty of acknowledging that an individual can be simultaneously acknowledged as a target of racism and as a perpetrator of injury was evident in the Clarence Thomas–Anita Hill story."[27] Here the defense of Thomas, the person perceived to be the target of racism, was used to evade discussion of misogyny and sexual harassment and to simultaneously discredit Hill's testimony. But Hill was also framed by the racist implication that black women are sexually available to all men and that this sexual degradation does not matter. This is what black feminist theorist Patricia Hill Collins calls "interlocking systems of oppression."[28]

Similarly, gay men and lesbians who are economically secure may be indifferent to the struggles of poor queer and trans people. Law enforcement officers of color who themselves have been targets of violence may be implicated in police violence. "Accountability remains," says Davis. "Victimization can no longer be permitted to function as a halo of innocence."

This halo of innocence should not hinder the ability to care about "less perfect" victims: the young, men of color who are framed by the media as thugs, women who are inebriated when they are sexually assaulted, people with arrest or school discipline records, or sex workers.

Rejecting this moral distancing moves society closer to acceptance of a better understanding of shared humanity. Accepting responsibility for addressing force that turns people into things is a necessary first step toward recognizing mass violence in its fullness.

THE DEATH OF TOM ROBINSON

To Kill a Mockingbird is one of the most heralded American stories of the twentieth century.[29] Harper Lee's novel won the 1960 Pulitzer Prize and has since sold more than thirty million copies. Many white people remember *Mockingbird* as the story that first opened their eyes to the terrible wrongs of racial injustice. Cultural and political scholars have examined the novel's representations of the racial dynamics and community life of fictional Maycomb, Alabama, and its exploration of the relation of social norms to questions of justice.[30]

To Kill a Mockingbird is one of the most regularly assigned books in school classrooms; it is also frequently banned from school libraries. The indictments, from both white and black people, progressives and conservatives, include: offensive themes and objectionable language; inappropriate sexual references to rape and incest; degrading portrayals of African Americans and people with cognitive disabilities; and incitements to race hatred against white people.

Lee's story was made into an acclaimed 1962 Academy Award–winning film. A near-the-top perennial on the American Film Institute's lists of the one hundred greatest and most inspiring movies, *To Kill a Mockingbird* is the coming-of-age story of Scout Finch, a young white girl, in the segregated South during the Great Depression, and the role that two men play in expanding her moral awareness. One of them is her mysterious and seldom-seen neighbor Boo Radley. The other is her father, Atticus Finch, a widower, who takes on the unpopular task of defending Tom Robinson, an apparently kind and humble black man falsely charged with the rape of a white woman.

Political and cultural debates about the merits and meaning of the novel and film have occurred for years. *Mockingbird* is a living thing, a creative work that has no fixed meaning in the public imagination. Imagination itself is a living thing as well. It is capable of shrinking and going stale, seeking only the comforting certainty of what readers already believe. Conversely, it can awaken new connections and fresh ways to revisit old dilemmas. *Mockingbird* holds new and unexpected relevance for understanding and educating about the necessity of moving beyond the hate frame.

In 1990, writing about whiteness and the literary imagination, Toni Morrison referred to the "strategic use of black characters to define the goals and enhance the qualities of white characters" in stories created by white writers, and noted how these writers manipulate imaginative encounters with black characters "as a means of meditation—both safe and risky—on one's own humanity."[31]

The reader of *Mockingbird* knows almost nothing about Tom Robinson apart from the limited interactions he has with white people in response to the accusation against him. Robinson is innocent of the charges. But *Mockingbird* is really a story about white people and Robinson exists to define the ethics and consciences of the white characters.

Novelist Thomas Mallon suggests that Lee's story "requires Tom Robinson's conviction as surely as the town itself does. Without it, the reader will not have the chance, like the Negroes in the balcony, to stand up and salute Atticus's nobly futile defense."[32] Tom Robinson does not exist on his own terms; he serves to illuminate the exemplary moral goodness of Atticus Finch. Robinson also functions as a human Rorschach test by which other white people are judged as good or bigoted. It is a crude measurement.

Finch's neighbor Miss Maudie, Sheriff Heck Tate, and Finch's children are also good white people. They disapprove of Bob Ewell, recognize the injustice to Tom Robinson, believe that everyone deserves a fair trial, and oppose lynching.

In contrast to these good white people are poor, uneducated whites represented as the primary purveyors of racism. They make false accusations against honest black people and attempt to form a lynch mob. Bob Ewell, the father, and real rapist, of Mayella, the woman whom Robinson purportedly assaulted, is the archetypal embodiment of evil. His greatest sin, however, is to threaten white children. Walter Cunningham, a poor farmer, represents a less toxic white man who helps instigate the lynch mob. Basically a good and decent man, he is momentarily swept up in the mob's force until he is shamed back into his right mind by Scout's spontaneous, simple words.

The liberal imagination frequently holds that violent racism is the exclusive province of ignorant bigots. This theme resonates throughout *Mockingbird*. It creates moral distance for white audiences, allowing them to bond around recognition of individual acts of racism and to condemn them. But this viewpoint never confronts more complicated expressions of racism and related questions of culpability.

When the incipient lynch mob has broken up, Atticus tells the children that it wasn't really a violent gang: "Those were our friends." He is right: ordinary people in unremarkable communities have always made up lynch mobs. Yet Finch goes on to dismiss the Klan as a group whose heyday has come and gone and no longer threatens anyone in

Maycomb. In the 1930s world of *Mockingbird*, the suggestion remains that as long as Bob Ewell is dead and Atticus Finch keeps watch over his children, the mob will never form again.

Tom Robinson is dead as well, killed by law enforcement officers as he tries to escape. He dies because he doesn't believe Atticus Finch's ludicrous belief that he would have a good chance on appeal. A man falsely accused, he must be shot dead to serve the story, even as law enforcement lies about who killed Bob Ewell so that Boo Radley, a white man, also essentially innocent, can go free.

Atticus Finch, Miss Maudie, Aunt Alexandria, Heck Tate, and the white children take note of Tom Robinson's death, their lives intact. Robinson's widow and children and Maycomb's entire black community are left to fend for themselves in a Jim Crow society where legal and extralegal violence blend seamlessly.

To Kill a Mockingbird has become a classic because of these messages. Historically, of course, as the book ends and the final film credits roll, the mob continues to form.

From 1882 to 1968, an estimated 4,700 people were lynched in the United States, most of whom were black men.[33] It was an extralegal form of execution openly or tacitly supported by local law enforcement. Lynching was a form of popularly supported, community-based violence designed to intimidate black people and keep them in their place. Often staged as public spectacles, the killings galvanized the civic imagination and carried enduring cultural force.

School officials sometimes canceled or delayed classes so students could attend the murder, or at least view its final result. The involvement of religious leaders, public officials, and community members was documented by Ida B. Wells, journalist and organizer who labored relentlessly in the late nineteenth century to mobilize opposition to lynching.[34]

Intervention or opposition by authorities was rare. Photographers and editorial cartoonists memorialized lynching; many of the popular images that document the horror were featured on postcards.[35]

Theologian James H. Cone notes the profound symbolic resonance of both the Christian cross and the lynching tree for many African Americans:

> One is the universal symbol of Christian faith; the other is the quintessential symbol of black oppression in America. Though both are symbols of death, one represents a message of hope and salvation, while the other signifies the negation of that message by white supremacy. Despite the obvious similarities between Jesus' death on a cross and the death of thousands of black men and women strung up to die on a lamppost or tree, relatively few people, apart from black poets, novelists, and other reality-seeing artists have explored the symbolic connections.[36]

The United States has still not explored those symbolic connections, historically, culturally, educationally, or politically, nor begun to come to terms with the magnitude of violence inflicted. Most people do not know how often those who were lynched were first stripped, raped or sodomized, whipped, castrated, and mutilated as part of a ritual of community cleansing that possessed an almost religious significance.

The mob that remains alive after *Mockingbird* ends goes on to assassinate black leaders, bomb churches, and murder children. Most of the people who do these things are not stereotypical rednecks. In *Carry Me Home*, an account of the civil rights struggle in Birmingham, Alabama in 1963, Diane McWhorter, who is white, charts the collusion of city leaders in resisting, too often violently, racial justice activism.

Mob mentality always reappears in a different form. It may be labeled a hate crime or seen in the appalling number of incidents in which police kill unarmed men of color. Sometimes the mob is found in homes. In the predawn hours of a November morning in 2013, a young black woman, nineteen-year-old Renisha McBride, who has been in a car accident and is bleeding and disoriented, knocks on the door of a Dearborn Heights, Michigan residence. Standing fewer than two feet away, the homeowner who opens the door shoots her in the face.

In 1962 Lillian Smith wrote that a mob isn't determined by the size of the crowd, because it is a state of mind that wants to hurt somebody. "Two or three people, even one can become a mob," she writes. Describing the white people who targeted Charlayne Hunter, one of the first two black students admitted to the University of Georgia in Athens, Smith argues they were behaving symbolically:

Did those students who threw stones at [her] hate the girl as a real individual? Did they know her? Had they ever talked to her? No. But she had come into their lives and her presence had become a profound threat to them. Now how was she threatening them? I can understand it only in this way: Charlayne Hunter, whom they did not know, was threatening them because she had become a ghost. . . . This young freshman had without knowing it become Someone who stands for Something Else. Suddenly she was a symbol of images, impulses, feelings, memories they dreaded; she was the ghost who embodies these dreads.[37]

What people seek to exclude or protect themselves against comes to define what they mean by justice. This in turn reinforces strategies of inclusion and exclusion—and the boundaries they establish. Often those boundaries constitute moral and ethical catastrophe.

A KNOCK AT THE DOOR

The idea of collective moral engagement feels overwhelming. Only through such engagement can transformative ideas about justice, responsibility, and public goodness emerge. The idea of the Neighbor is a place to begin. The politics of fear portrays the Neighbor as harassing and intruding. "What increasingly emerges as the central human right in late-capitalist society," Slavoj Zizek remarks, "is *the right not to be harassed*, which is a right to remain at a safe distance from others.

The proximity of people who suffer torture, he contends, brings these undesirables too close to us. This proximity, conceptual and symbolic, is evoked through ethical concern for the well-being of the Neighbor. But the Neighbor has largely been banished from the civic conscience, the public imagination. In an attempt to destroy this proximity, American society may be attempting "nothing less than *the abolition of the dimension of the Neighbour*."[38] It is essential to reverse that process and openly claim proximity as an impetus to collective moral engagement.

In the summer of 1967, less than a year before he was assassinated, the Reverend Martin Luther King Jr. delivered a sermon, "A Knock at Midnight."[39] Focusing on the role of the church in grappling with contemporary injustices and anxieties, King's sermon drew its inspiration from a verse in the Gospel of Luke: "Which of you who has a friend will go to him at midnight and say to him, 'Friend, lend me three loaves; for a friend of mine has arrived on a journey, and I have nothing to set before him'?" (Luke 11:5–6).

Today's weary sojourner seeks the bread of faith: the faith of spiritual and ethical meaning, in one's neighbors, and in the future. The sojourner seeks the bread of hope and the bread of love—not merely love for one's family, but the love made tangible through authentic forms of social and economic justice.

But the knock comes at midnight where paralyzing fears and anxieties "harrow people by day and haunt them by night." And the knock comes at midnight when the eleventh commandment, "Thou shalt not get caught," too often substitutes for justice. One might even hate in this moral order, Dr. King asserts, so long as that hate is hypocritically disguised as love. Midnight is a confusing, dispiriting time when the temptation to relinquish belief in meaningful change—the possibility that things could not only be different, but dramatically better—is great.

And yet midnight is also precisely the time when persistence produces astonishing transformation. In Luke, the homeowner responds with an impatient refusal: "I cannot get up and give you anything." But the parable's lesson is that the traveler must never consent to that indifference; must boldly continue to assert the need for sustenance—food, justice, and compassionate community. The door will open, perhaps in surprising ways. A different result is possible. Different relationships, more compassionate and just, can come into existence.

It is necessary to hold to that belief today, when the knock at midnight is likely to be met with the blast of rhetorical and actual guns fired by angry, frightened people—civilians, political leaders, corporate moguls, police, and soldiers—all standing our ground in a world of suspicion and enmity.

5

GOODNESS IN THE
PUBLIC IMAGINATION

"That you can't fight City Hall, is a rumor
being spread by City Hall."

—AUDRE LORDE

It is impossible for society to move forward if it cannot first imagine
a different and better future. Imagination, the ability to confront and
remake reality by utilizing creative powers of mind and spirit, is an essential but undervalued political tool. It does not replace activism and
community organizing, but inspires and animates it. It brings new an-
alytical insight into being. It invigorates new social understandings of
goodness, justice, and moral agency. It gives these concepts symbolic
meaning and changes the terms of public discourse and debate. At its
most powerful it challenges American culture to go beyond superficial
reform that leaves the status quo intact. In *The Prophetic Imagination*
(1978), Biblical scholar Walter Brueggemann argues that imagination
evokes the language of newness and radical hope, which is antithetical
to the ethos of domination.

A CONTEST OF IMAGINATIONS

Political activism, both right and left, is frequently viewed through a lens of enmity: the triumph or defeat of the enemy is what is at stake.

This is not new. People have always more easily motivated themselves and others through fear than through positive visions of change. It is much easier to shut down hearts and minds through suspicion, resentment, and loathing than to open them.

President George W. Bush summed this up in his post-9/11 national security strategy, which permits launching a preemptive war whenever the nation feels threatened. "Defending our Nation against its enemies is the first and fundamental commitment of the Federal Government," he declared.[1] The stand-your-ground legitimation of civilian killings by other, fearful civilians also embodies this worldview. So do public policies that seek, in the name of safety, to arm people in public schools and other civic venues. It is an ethical orientation that simultaneously arises from and buttresses the hate frame.

Lawrence Thornton underscored the reality of a state imagination rooted in violence and oppression in his 1987 novel *Imagining Argentina*. Set in the late 1970s, when that nation was controlled by a brutal military dictatorship, it tells the story of Carlos Rueda, whose wife is among the thousands of people, considered enemies of the state, who have been disappeared. Rueda develops the gift of "seeing," in waking dreams, the fates of those who have vanished. As he tells the stories of what he sees, some of the disappeared are returned to their loved ones. Imagination has the power to alter reality.

One day, as he watches security agents of the dictatorship drive by, Rueda explains the necessity for a contest of imaginations to his friend Silvio: "So long as we accept what the men in the car imagine, we're finished. All I've been trying to tell you is that there are two

Argentinas, Silvio, the regime's travesty of it, and the one we have in our hearts. . . .We have to believe in the power of imagination because it is all we have, and ours is stronger than theirs."[2]

What is always at stake in a contest of imaginations is the question of whose lives matter. Deep cultural and structural change is impossible to achieve when racing from issue to issue and crisis to crisis, seeing each issue and crisis as separate and distinct. To do so is to remain within the imagination of the dominant culture. Transformative imagination refuses those constraints; it invites people to think differently and more boldly about the interrelatedness of issues and concerns. It precedes policy proposals and offers fresh perspectives on how individual and collective change occurs by breaking through the paralysis of despair and hopelessness. It has deeply practical potential for mobilizing people across issues and movements.

MADRES DE PLAZA DE MAYO

The Argentinian military dictatorship came into power in 1976 through the armed overthrow and exile of the president, Isabel Perón; it ruled until 1983. During this period, thousands of people were abducted, tortured, and killed. Over three hundred detention centers dotted the country. An estimated five hundred children belonging to those who were disappeared were given to the families of high-ranking officers and public officials to raise as their own.[3]

The women who created the Madres de Plaza de Mayo (Mothers of the May Plaza) met one another as they searched, with no success, for their missing sons and daughters.[4] The junta claimed it had no information. At first, the women met quietly, exchanged information, and tried not to call attention to themselves. In time, a small number of the Madres made their witness public, walking slowly in a circle around Plaza de Mayo. Plans for a weekly gathering and walk began to take shape. They also continued to write letters seeking help in finding their children and to circulate petitions demanding accountability from the junta.

Initially, there were no protest banners, only white baby shawls or headscarves on which the mothers inscribed the names of their children. The scarves made visible their loss and served as a symbol of a mother's love. In witnessing, they refashioned the image of a good mother from one who is obedient, silent, and submissive into a public vision of goodness: a determined mother who never stops caring about her children and is willing to demonstrate that publicly.

Over time, the gatherings grew into the hundreds. People carried banners and photos of the disappeared. Where the dictatorship imposed erasure, the response was public remembrance.

The Madres risked arrest and abuse; at one point about a dozen members of the group were permanently disappeared. Military police disrupted the gatherings by denying access to the plaza. The more these dignified mourners insisted on accountability from the authorities, the more the force deployed against them increased.

Throughout the dictatorship's rule, the Madres constituted the most visible Argentinian expression of resistance. Their actions symbolically dismantled the violence of the military authorities. Even as they refused the junta's assumptions about what constituted public order, they did not align with specific political parties, but were an independent moral voice. In 1982, a March of Resistance called by the Madres de Plaza de Mayo attracted thousands.

In a bleak and frightening time, the Madres shifted public consciousness. They did not avoid fear but moved closer to it. In doing so they transformed themselves and a nation.

THE DEATH OF AMY BIEHL

The transformative possibilities of imagination can also be seen in what happened in 1993 and beyond in the black township of Gugulethu in Cape Town, South Africa.

In late summer, Amy Biehl, a twenty-six-year-old white American Fulbright scholar studying the role of women in transitional regimes, was driving several black colleagues to their homes. An active supporter of the African National Congress, she worked with the black-led resistance to the violence of South Africa's institutionalized racism. As Biehl slowly motored her way through the area, an angry crowd formed, throwing stones and shouting antiwhite slogans. In the mob's mind, Amy embodied the very real brutality of white Afrikaner rule. A brick hit the car's windshield. The car stopped, and Amy Biehl was stoned and stabbed to death.

This violence occurred in the dying days of white Afrikaner apartheid. In 1990, after Nelson Mandela was released from prison, new elections were scheduled to be held the following year. Even with change on the horizon, South African blacks remained at the mercy of the apartheid regime. Between Mandela's release and his subsequent election as president four years later, over ten thousand people, most of them black, died as a result of state violence.[5]

Four young South African men were convicted of Amy Biehl's murder and sent to prison. Several years into their sentences, they appeared before the postapartheid Truth and Reconciliation Commission.[6] This government body, established by the South African parliament in 1995, oversaw a transitional justice process to address the massive human rights abuses of apartheid.[7] The men who killed Biehl petitioned for amnesty. Despite their grief, Linda and Peter Biehl, Amy's parents, supported the petition. The men were released in 1998.

Despite its many limitations, the Truth and Reconciliation Commission sought to embody the imagination necessary to envision an alternative to vengeance.[8] Biehl's parents shared this vision, honoring Amy's humanity even as they refused to lose sight of the humanity of those who killed her. This expression of goodness held the potential for transformation. In 1994 Amy's parents had established the nonprofit Amy Biehl Foundation to serve the children of the impoverished townships of the Western Cape.

A related expression of goodness was made by two of the young men, Easy Nofemela and Ntobeko Peni, both just nineteen years old when they killed Amy. Following their release from prison, Nofemela and Peni joined the Amy Biehl Foundation staff. This organization now provides afterschool programs and opportunities—HIV/AIDS peer education, literacy, music and the performing arts, sports, and environmental activities—crucial to helping boys and girls in the Western Cape create better futures by helping to understand themselves as good, talented, responsible people, members of larger communities.

The murder of Amy Biehl and its aftermath contradict the hate frame in multiple ways. One person is murdered. Four other people, whose lives are forever linked to hers, collide in horrific circumstances. Those four people come to recognize one another as worthy human beings. The violence of apartheid touches each of them in different but interdependent, ways. Refusing to compete for primary victim status or the righteousness of a particular animus, they understand the nature of the violence that engulfs them and assume responsibility for what happens next. In time, they transform themselves and one another.

The outcome of this one story did not solve the injustices that continue to exist in postapartheid South Africa. Nor did the Truth and Reconciliation Commission produce justice for all. Nelson Mandela's presidency and subsequent black-led administrations could not, in a relatively short time, substantially dismantle a historically entrenched culture of violence. Though the formal structures of apartheid are gone and many important changes have been enacted, economic power remains largely in white hands. Black poverty remains widespread. Violence has not disappeared.

Nonetheless, as these events demonstrate, mandates for vengeance can be transformed into practices that strengthen communities instead of tearing them apart. This is not done by authority figures but by us, the ordinary people. Permitting those already in charge to determine the terms of debate will never produce real change.

TOWARD TRANSFORMATION AND JUSTICE

How can justice practices shift from a focus on vengeance to an emphasis on healing, reparation, and transformation of the conditions that produce violence?

To imagine this possibility, those who do serious harm to others must hold themselves accountable for their actions and work to repair the harm they have caused. None of this must come at the expense of those they have harmed, and the safety, healing, and agency of survivors must be emphasized. Healing and transformation is also possible for those who commit acts of violence.

In 2010 Conor McBride, a nineteen-year-old white man, turned himself in to the Tallahassee, Florida, police department, an hour after he shot his girlfriend, Ann Margaret Grosmaire, also nineteen, in the face at point-blank range.[9] She died four days later. The couple had been fighting for two days.

Ann Margaret Grosmaire's parents, Kate and Andy, expected their daughter and McBride would marry. At the hospital, before Ann

Margaret died, her father believed he heard her voice saying, "Forgive him." He felt she was asking too much, but tried to act in accordance with that message. Kate Grosmaire later said, "Before this happened, I loved Conor. I knew that if I defined [him] by that one moment—as a murderer—I was defining my daughter as a murder victim. And I could not allow that to happen."

The prosecutor was surprised to learn the Grosmaires did not want McBride to spend the rest of his life in prison, and reluctantly agreed to an alternative process, with elements of restorative justice, reserving the right to make the final sentencing recommendation.

There are many different approaches to restorative justice, but it generally seeks to replace the adversarial nature of legal proceedings with a survivor-centered focus on the harm that has been done. The goal is that those who do harm will acknowledge the full impact of their actions, and agree to make amends or repair the harm to the extent possible.[10]

Andy and Kate Grosmaire, Conor McBride, his parents, and the prosecutor met with a facilitator. A photograph of Ann Grosmaire ensured her presence. For the first time, the Grosmaires heard McBride's own detailed account of the events leading to their daughter's murder. McBride did not excuse anything he'd done as he described the mix of exhaustion, frustration, confusion, and rage that he felt before shooting Ann. He held himself fully accountable. Both sets of parents also spoke. The group discussed possible sentencing options.

The prosecutor consulted community leaders before making his final recommendation. Though the Grosmaires asked for a shorter sentence, McBride agreed to a twenty-year sentence plus an additional ten years of probation during which he will help educate others about teen dating violence. Since his incarceration, he has worked in the prison's law library, taken steps to address his anger, maintained strong connections with his own family and the Grosmaires, and started making plans for the future.

This new vision of justice offers hope for moving beyond a framework of vengeance.

Beyond restorative justice, other alternative approaches called healing justice, transformational justice, and community-centered justice exist. They focus on survivor well-being, support, agency, reparation, and healing, for both individuals and entire communities, and also on accountability and voluntary, constructive transformation for those who do harm to others. Emphasis is placed on strengthening community accountability for violence—outside the criminal legal system and without resort to vigilante tactics. Collective action to address the social and economic conditions that give rise to violence is promoted. American Indian and other indigenous peoples throughout the world traditionally have addressed fractures in "right relationship"—that is, elements of relationship that are untrustworthy, degrading, exploitative, or abusive—through practices that focus on healing and good outcomes for all affected by or implicated in the harm, including the wider community.[11]

These alternatives to the criminal legal system focus on the creation of just and constructive relationships that reflect an understanding of shared humanity, taking into account both individual and collective realities.

DISRUPTIVE INTELLIGENCE AND TRANSFORMATIVE IMAGINATION

The world is articulated again and again through the creative agency of individuals and societies. Society itself can be considered a product of imagination. Society's structures are symbolic as well as functional, affecting individual as well as collective consciousness. "World-image and self-image are obviously always related."[12]

The dominant American imagination thinks about violence, goodness, guilt, innocence, and justice in four primary ways:

Enemy orientation: structuring society and culture to identify, contain, and eliminate enemies. There is a constant expansion of those regarded as troublemakers to be excluded or controlled. Fear and suspicion serve to rationalize violence and oppression. Safety is contingent upon the deployment of surveillance and the maintenance of impermeable borders. Policing and militarization extend into education and social services. Justice is equated with retribution, vengeance, incarceration, and control.

Supremacist assumptions: structuring society and culture to reinforce assumptions about the superiority of some categories of people and the inferiority of others. The institutionalization of these beliefs leads to systemic processes of degradation, discrimination, criminalization, exclusion, and violence. These assumptions maintain traditional and unjust racial, gender, and class hierarchies, which are regarded as eternal, natural, and inevitable. Antiblack racism is the "fulcrum of white supremacy," in the US, even though other communities of color also experience the harms of racism.[13]

Unregulated markets and consumer commodification: promoting the acquisition of things and regarding markets, rather than governance accountable to its people, as the primary means for fostering freedom. This mindset reduces all aspects of life—human beings, animal and plant life, shared natural resources, even justice—to commodities: things that are bought, sold, and privatized. Cultural critic Lewis Hyde has noted that corporations have snapped up ideas and art that once belonged to a larger cultural commons. "The loyalty of school children, indigenous knowledge, drinking water, the human genome—it's all for sale," he says.[14] There is a steady transfer of public revenues and resources into private corporations. Public spaces and civic venues, including schools, are removed from public stewardship and accountability. The primary beneficiaries are those who are already wealthy. Pursuit of profit always takes precedence over public well-being.

Individualism repudiates the reality of interdependence and negates shared responsibility, the Commons, and the common good. Justice is individualized and unevenly enforced. Public and private institutions are rarely held accountable for harm they cause. The impacts of violence and inequalities are attributed to the character flaws and moral failings of individuals or groups.[15]

These elements of the dominant American imagination are at the core of what writer Sarah Schulman identifies as "the centerpiece of supremacy ideology, the idea that one person's life is more important than another's," and "the gentrification of the mind."[16]

Transformation is made possible only by refusing to accept the elements of the dominant imagination as the only available terms of debate. This cannot be accomplished by political action and language alone. Imaginative and energizing forms of cultural expression are also required: images, symbols, characters, stories, poems, music, and whatever else can touch the entire person, including the senses, the unconscious, and the heart. Their purpose is to offer upsetting insights and utilize "disruptive intelligence" to disturb "the established categories of truth and property."[17]

Disruptive intelligence is not a hectoring, accusatory means of shifting blame, nor does it seek to transfer repressive authority to another group. As Hyde writes, if it simply mirrors that which it opposes, disruptive intelligence is incapable of charting alternative paths into new worlds. Even as it dismantles old paradigms, it must also be about the work of opening doorways into spaces filled with fresh possibility.

Disruptive intelligence shines unexpected and surprising spotlights on society's shibboleths and fictions so that people can view them less defensively. It appears in any guise, as high art, low comedy, or spiritual teaching. It may make us laugh or rend our hearts. It may show up as a prophetic presence, breaking through political jargon to reveal deeper truths or point to contradictions between what is promised and what is given. Since transformation requires structural shifts, disruptive intelligence almost always finds ways to highlight a society's many convoluted boundaries, created in increasingly desperate quests for safety, and then intentionally violate them.

The telling of disruptive and unsettling truth in American society begins with exposing lies told about safety and what is necessary to secure it. As James Baldwin said, "Art is here to prove, and to help one bear, the fact that all safety is an illusion."[18]

It is natural that people want caring, affirming communities in which to live, where we can flourish and thrive. But American society focuses primarily on fear and exclusion, not on the positive creation of caring and just communities, and seeks safety primarily through intensified policing. This results in "a state of being that might best be described as protectionist (or perhaps isolationist)."[19] In the end, such strategies encourage a kind of withdrawal from the larger society, a repudiation of the Neighbor, and a tolerance of violence. They drive people deeper into the confines of prisons of mind, spirit, and social structure.

Disruptive elements of a transformative American imagination, by contrast, are potentially limitless. Because they are inherently unpredictable, fluid, and part of a larger creative commons, no can assert ownership of them. But they might include these:

Radical and compassionate embrace of the Neighbor: This constitutes a commitment to community well-being that is capable of acting selflessly for the benefit of the Other. "We shrug off, shake off, walk away from, close our eyes to the world of unhappiness," says psychiatrist Robert Coles.[20] Counterintuitively, this radical embrace requires us to move toward, rather than away from, the pain and suffering of others—especially strangers. This brings us closer to a real experience of shared humanity.

Forthrightly facing, and not minimizing, pain is an essential part of healing that, Robert Jay Lifton claims, holds the possibility of transformation:

You look into the abyss, but you don't want to be stuck there. Otherwise your imagination is deadened and defeated. . . . So you want to look into it in order to see beyond it. If you don't look into it, you are ostrich-like. If you get stuck there, you're incapacitated. So you want to look beyond it to other human possibilities.[21]

This is what inspired Thomas DeWolf, a white man whose ancestors controlled the largest slave-trading dynasty in US history, and Sharon Morgan, a black woman who is descended from slaves on both sides of her family, to embark on a three-year journey of dialogue and travel. Their purpose was to better understand the deep social wounds inherited from a violent racial past in order to discern possibilities for individual and collective healing. Their odyssey required them to confront the legacies of slavery and racism in their own lives and the larger society. They made a commitment to take action to address persistent and traumatic legacies of slavery, including race-based economic and health disparities and mass incarceration.[22]

Such approaches provide antidotes to indifference, a preoccupation with self-protection, and isolation. They also require more than sentimental good wishes and a theoretical appreciation of diversity. Community well-being is not created on an individual basis, but by establishing and nurturing just, trustworthy relationships in society even when people resist them. These relationships cannot exist when the parameters are dictated by the dominant culture. Howard Thurman, an influential religious leader of the twentieth century, reminds us of the expansive nature of true neighborliness and community that extends beyond human beings: "It is worth noting that from time immemorial men have felt that there was a universal language prior to the creation of symbols of communication such as words. This language included all living things."[23]

An ethic of public goodness demands that people make new efforts to increase moral awareness of what is happening to our Neighbor, to ask more questions, and to act in light of new awareness. As an antidote to enmity, isolation, and exclusion in times of uncertainty and fear, author Barry Lopez proposes a more expansive and engaged idea of conversation with the Neighbor:

> Conversations are efforts toward good relations. They are an elementary form of reciprocity. They are the exercise of our love for each other. They are the enemies of our loneliness, our doubt, our anxiety, our tendencies to abdicate. To continue to be in good conversation over our enormous and terrifying problems is to be calling out to each other in the night. If we attend with imagination and devotion to our conversations, we will find what

we need; and someone among us will act—it does not matter whom—and we will survive.[24]

An ethic of interdependence and accountability: This recognizes how one action affects and alters other things and requires a commitment to be answerable to one another for the impacts of our words and actions. It is the opposite of an ethos of rugged individualism; it recognizes how actions have ripple effects on individuals, communities, and the environment. It requires taking action to tend to and ensure the well-being and sustainability of all. This element of disruptive imagination repudiates the ideology of supremacy in its specific structural and cultural manifestations.

Commitment to expansion of the Commons: This affirms that all people must have ready access, without economic hardship, to resources necessary to create a sustainable future. These include natural resources, public spaces, communications technologies, and essential civic supports such as housing, food, education, and health care. Such a shift would be a repudiation of the complete privatization of lands, resources, and public services, many of which were once held in common. It is a public declaration that no one is expendable and we all belong.

In 2013 the Moral Monday Movement, a vibrant expression of alternative consciousness, was created to challenge North Carolina Republicans, who had taken over the state legislature in 2010.[25] The new legislative majority had shifted money from public education to vouchers for private schools, stopped federal unemployment benefits, and slashed taxes for the wealthy while raising them for others. Moral Monday, a multiracial, multi-issue movement voicing expansive concepts of social and economic justice, emerged. During its first year, they held rallies and staged direct actions at the state capitol and in thirty cities. Powered by transformative joy as well as street protests, Moral Monday mounted legal challenges to the state's voter suppression law and worked to register voters. In early 2014, near the fifty-fourth anniversary of a lunch counter sit-in by four black students at North Carolina A & T in support of desegregation, a Moral March held in Raleigh attracted at least eighty thousand people.

The first step toward a transformed future is to speak out for it, to refuse to remain silent; to challenge all of the feelings and forces that encourage people to remain mired in resentment, cynicism, fear, and despair. In 1977 Audre Lorde, identifying herself as a black lesbian poet, activist, and mother, spoke of the life-giving necessity of transforming silence into language and action: "We can sit mute in our corners forever while our sisters and ourselves are wasted, while our children are distorted and destroyed, while our earth is poisoned; we can sit in our safe corners mute as bottles, and we will be no less afraid."[26]

It is less our differences, profound though they are, that so often immobilize us. The deepest paralysis is a silence policed by fear, that is not only external, but which we internalize within ourselves.

PUBLIC GOODNESS

The core challenge in all of this is transformation of the American imagination. Without this, it is almost impossible to foster public embrace of collective responsibility. Meeting the challenge requires new ways of understanding goodness within compelling frameworks that expand the imaginative possibilities for enacting justice.

Mishuana Goeman's *Mark My Words: Native Women Mapping Our Nations* creates one such framework. Utilizing twentieth-century Native women's poetry and prose, she repudiates and (re)maps "colonial [settler] organizing of land, bodies, and social and political landscapes."

Imaginative modes, she points out, provide "avenues beyond a recovery of a violent history of erasure" and can disrupt the dominant culture's histories and violent frameworks for imposing order.[27] Disruptive insight, so central to transformative imagination, suggests that where the dominant culture erases peoples, the tasks are to publicly notice the erasure and to grieve those who are lost, to remember them, and to repopulate the world by bringing them to life again. Where history is lost or distorted, the task is to retell the stories outside of dominant frameworks.

Where structural inequalities and violence are in ascendance, the task is to refuse their "inevitability," to repudiate them with new stories of what is possible through a public ethic of compassion and shared resources. Disruptive insight pokes gaping holes in the official story by offering unexpected narratives, images, and symbols that envision a significantly better future as well as ethical ways of achieving it.

Deep down, most people are aware of the stale, self-serving nature of most political discourse. By accepting the existing culture's assumptions, movements for progressive change will never move beyond them. It is the difference between a movement to abolish slavery and one predicated on the reforming of slavery's worst abuses, or at least hiding them better.

In 2012, in a lecture given at Harvard Divinity School, Toni Morrison examined the treatment of the concept of goodness in the literary imagination. "Goodness in contemporary literature," she said, "always seems to be equated with weakness" while evil commandeers the public platform. But in her own work, she makes sure that expressions of goodness are never incidental, never trivial. "In fact," she said, "I want them to have life-changing properties and to illuminate decisively the moral questions embedded in the narrative."[28]

That is the task of transformative imagination.

It is not necessary to be an artist to engage this work. The abolitionists who risked their lives running the Underground Railroad and the women at the center of the 1955 Montgomery, Alabama, bus boycott that led to a US Supreme Court ruling declaring segregation on public buses to be unconstitutional were ordinary community residents. So were the Madres of Buenos Aires.

This is an undertaking that promises both possibility and pain. It is impossible to explore questions of goodness without a willingness to witness, examine, and resist brutality and inhumanity. There is no automatic relationship between transformative imagination and progressive political and social change. Without disruptive intelligence that seeks a transformation of consciousness, no lasting structural change is possible.

Every age engages in a complex negotiation between existing power structures and emergent ideas about human possibility. The most emancipatory ideas, translated however imperfectly into cultural expression and activism, become lifelines for future generations.

FOR FURTHER EXPLORATION:
BOOKS, FILMS, AND COMMUNITY RESOURCES

For a more in-depth exploration of some of the topics discussed in this book, the authors recommend the following resources, most of which are not directly cited in the text. The emphasis is on resources intended to stir moral, political, and cultural imagination.

BOOKS

Rita Nakashima Brock and Gabriella Lettini, *Soul Repair: Recovering from Moral Injury After War* (Boston: Beacon, 2013).

Walter Brueggemann, *The Practice of Prophetic Imagination: Preaching an Emancipating Word* (Minneapolis, MN: Fortress, 2012).

Ann Cvetkovich, *An Archive of Feelings: Trauma, Sexuality, and Lesbian Public Cultures* (Durham, NC: Duke University Press, 2003).

Edwidge Danticat, *Create Dangerously: The Immigrant Artist at Work* (New York: Vintage, 2011).

Angela Y. Davis, *Are Prisons Obsolete?* (New York: Seven Stories, 2003).

Lewis Hyde, *The Gift: Creativity and the Artist in the Modern World* (New York: Vintage, 2007).

Sarah Schulman, *The Gentrification of the Mind: Witness to a Lost Generation* (Berkeley: University of California Press, 2013).

Susan Sontag, *Regarding the Pain of Others* (New York: Farrar, Straus, and Giroux, 2003).

Simone Weil, *Oppression and Liberty* (Amherst, MA: University of Massachusetts Press, 1978).

DOCUMENTARY FILMS

Herman's House, directed by Angad Bhalla, produced by Lisa Valencia-Svensson, Ed Barreveld, and Loring McAlpin, 2012. http://hermanshousethe film.com/the-film/.

> Herman Wallace died in 2013, having served forty-one years in solitary confinement in a Louisiana prison. What kind of house does a man who has been imprisoned in a six-foot-by-nine-foot cell for four decades dream of? This film captures the remarkable creative journey and friendship of Herman Wallace and artist Jackie Sumell while examining the inhumanity of prolonged solitary confinement.

No! The Rape Documentary, produced and directed by Aishah Shahidah Simmons. AfroLez Productions, 2006. http://notherapedocumentary.org/ sexual-assault-documentary-no.

> A groundbreaking, award-winning documentary featuring riveting testimonials from black women rape survivors who defy victimization. A supplemental video, *Breaking the Silence*, and study guide, *Unveiling the Silence*, are also available.

United in Anger: A History of ACT UP, directed by Jim Hubbard, produced by Jim Hubbard and Sarah Schulman, 2012.

> An inspiring documentary "from the perspective of those in the trenches" about the birth and life of the AIDS activist movement. Utilizing oral histories and rare archival footage, the film depicts the efforts of ACT UP (AIDS Coalition to Unleash Power) as it battles corporate greed, social indifference, and government negligence. A study guide is available.

COMMUNITY RESOURCES: HEALING, TRANSFORMATIVE, AND RESTORATIVE JUSTICE

Community Accountability: Emerging Movements to Transform Violence, a special issue of *Social Justice: A Journal of Crime, Conflict & World Order* 37, no. 4 (2011–12), critically examines grassroots efforts, cultural interventions, and theoretical questions regarding community-based strategies to address gendered violence. This collection encapsulates a decade of local and national initiatives, led or inspired by allied social movements, that reflect the complexities of integrating the theory and practice of community accountability. http://communityaccountability.wordpress.com/social-justice-journal -issue/article-downloads/.

Community accountability resources from INCITE! INCITE! http://www .incite-national.org/page/community-accountability.

Creative Interventions Toolkit: A Practical Guide to Stop Interpersonal Violence. Pre-release version. Creative Interventions, 2012. http://www.creative -interventions.org/tools/toolkit/.

Healing justice resources from American Friends Service Committee. https:// afsc.org/goal/healing-justice.

Toward Transformative Justice: A Liberatory Approach to Child Sexual Abuse and Other Forms of Intimate and Community Violence. Generation Five, 2007. http://www.generationfive.org/resources/transformative-justice-documents/.

Transformative justice resources recommended by Prison Culture blog. http://www.usprisonculture.com/blog/transformative-justice/.

Zehr Institute for Restorative Justice, an initiative of the Center for Justice and Peacebuilding at Eastern Mennonite University. http://www.emu.edu/cjp /restorative-justice/.

ACKNOWLEDGMENTS

Our collaborative work on *Considering Hate* has been enriched by the support, insight, and assistance of many. While responsibility for the final text is ours alone, we are grateful to Michael Amico, Amy Gottlieb, Nancy A. Heitzeg, and Joey L. Mogul for reviewing and commenting on particular sections of the manuscript.

We also want to thank the remarkable people at Beacon Press, including executive editor Gayatri Patnaik, who originally proposed the idea for this book and whose ideas have helped to shape it, as well as managing editor Susan Lumenello, assistant editor Rachael Marks, copyeditor Gary Von Euer, and cover designer Gabi Anderson. Thanks also go to Helene Atwan, Beacon's executive director; Tom Hallock, director of sales and marketing; Pam MacColl, communications director; and Caitlin Meyer and Travis Dagenais, publicists.

Kay also expresses gratitude to Pat Clark, Aishah Shahidah Simmons, Nancy A. Heitzeg, Ejeris Dixon, Gabriel Foster, Joey L. Mogul, Andrea J. Ritchie, Chip Berlet, Tarso Ramos, and Mariame Kaba, whose work and insights over the years have influenced this work. Thanks also to Seeta Persaud, Karla Saunders, Amy Hoffman, Debra Cash, and Rachael Kamel. My gratitude goes, as well, to organizations and blogs that have initiated, supported, and expanded critical discussions about the hate frame, including the American Friends Service Committee, Queers for Economic Justice, Barnard Center for Research on Women, Political Research Associates, Audre Lorde Project, Sylvia Rivera Law Project, FIERCE, TGI Justice Project, Community United Against Violence, Gender JUST, Against Equality, Transformative Justice Law Project of Illinois, Prison Culture, and Critical Mass Progress. Southerners on New Ground (SONG) and Astrea Lesbian Foundation for Justice claim special places in my political imagination. Finally, thanks to my beloved circle of friends and family who have offered such wonderful encouragement and support, especially my partner, Phoebe Hunter.

Michael thanks Michael Amico, Richard Voos, Alison Pirie, Ivy Schweitzer, Aubry Threlkeld, Joseph Canarelli, Sue Hyde, and Andrew Longhi.

NOTES

INTRODUCTION

1. See Donna Minkowitz, "Love and Hate in Laramie," *Nation*, July 12, 1999. See also JoAnn Wypijewski, "A Boy's Life: For Matthew Shepard's Killers, What Does It Take to Pass as a Man?" *Harper's*, September 1999, and Stephen Jimenez, *The Book of Matt: Hidden Truths About the Murder of Matthew Shepard* (Hanover, NH: Steerforth, 2013).

CHAPTER 1: DEHUMANIZATION AND VIOLENCE

Elizabeth Farnsworth interview with Toni Morrison on PBS NewsHour, March 9, 1998, http://www.pbs.org/newshour/bb/entertainment/jan -june98/morrison_3–9.html.

1. Other whites were also involved in the abduction and killing of Emmett Till, but no one else was charged. The two men acquitted of Till's murder later confessed in the pages of *Look* magazine, in an article written by William Bradford Huie, January 1956. Online at http://www.pbs.org/wgbh /amex/till/sfeature/sf_look_confession.html.

2. In 2012, according to the National Coalition of Anti-Violence Programs (NCAVP), almost 90 percent of anti-LGBTQ and HIV-affected homicide victims were people of color; about half were black/African American. Half also were transgender women, even though transgender survivors/ victims represent only about 10.5 percent of total reports to NCAVP. Transgender people were at demonstrably higher risk than cisgender (a term used to identify individuals whose gender identity and expression match the sex they were assigned at birth) people. See NCAVP, "Lesbian, Gay, Bisexual, Transgender, Queer and HIV-Affected Hate Violence in

2012" (2013 release edition), 8–9, http://www.avp.org/resources/avp
-resources/248.

3. For a powerful account of the killing of Marcelo Lucero and the social,
   political, and economic context in which it occurred, see Mirta Ojito,
   Hunting Season: Immigration and Murder in an All-American Town
   (Boston: Beacon Press, 2013).

4. Robert Bogdan, *Freak Show: Presenting Human Oddities for Amusement
   and Profit* (Chicago: University of Chicago Press, 1988), 146.

5. Edward J. Ingebretsen, *At Stake: Monsters and the Rhetoric of Fear in Public Culture* (Chicago: University of Chicago Press, 2001), 26.

6. Douglas C. Baynton, "Disability and the Justification of Inequality in
   American History," in *The Disability Studies Reader*, 4th edition, ed. Len-
   nard J. Davis (New York: Routledge, 2013), 17.

7. John M. Coward, *The Newspaper Indian: Native American Identity in the
   Press, 1820–90* (Urbana: University of Illinois Press, 1999), 46–47.

8. Andrea Smith, *Conquest: Sexual Violence and American Indian Genocide*
   (Cambridge, MA: South End Press, 1995), 8–10.

9. Coward, *The Newspaper Indian*, 65.

10. Toni Morrison, *Playing in the Dark: Whiteness in the Literary Imagination*
    (Cambridge, MA: Harvard University Press, 1992), 38.

11. Baynton, "Disability and the Justification of Inequality in American
    History," 17.

12. Mary Douglas, *Purity and Danger* (London: Routledge, 2002), 142. First
    published by Routledge, Keegan, Paul, 1966.

13. Ibid., 202.

14. Paul Ricoeur, *The Symbolism of Evil* (Boston: Beacon Press, 1969), 25.

15. A. O. Wright, "The Defective Classes," Proceedings of the National
    Conference of Charities and Correction (1891), 1. Available online at the
    Disability History Museum website, http://www.disabilitymuseum.org
    /dhm/lib/detail.html?id=2531&page=all.

16. Ricoeur, *Symbolism of Evil*, 25–26.

17. Wright, "The Defective Classes," 4.

18. David L. Lightner, *Asylum, Prison, and Poorhouse: The Writings and
    Reform Work of Dorothea Dix in Illinois* (Carbondale: Southern Illinois
    University Press, 1999), ix.

19. Robert Bogdan, *Freak Show: Presenting Human Oddities for Amusement
    and Profit* (Chicago: University of Chicago Press, 1988).

20. For a concise and powerful critical summary of Saartje Baartman's experience, see Christina Sharp, *Monstrous Intimacies: Making Post-Slavery Subjects* (Durham, NC: Duke University Press, 2010), 67–109.

21. Nicole Hahn Rafter, *Creating Born Criminals* (Urbana: University of Illinois Press, 1997).

22. Cesare Lombroso, *Criminal Man*, trans. and with a new introduction by Mary Gibson and Nicole Hahn Rafter (Durham, NC: Duke University Press, 2006). This is a compendium of material from all five editions.

23. Cesare Lombroso and Guglielmo Ferrero, *Criminal Woman, the Prostitute, and the Normal Woman*, trans. and with a new introduction by Nicole Hahn Rafter and Mary Gibson (Durham, NC: Duke University Press, 2004).

24. Eithne Luibhéid, *Entry Denied: Controlling Sexuality at the Border* (Minneapolis: University of Minnesota Press, 2002), xiii.

25. Madison Grant, *The Passing of the Great Race or the Racial Basis of European History* (New York: Charles Scribner's Sons, 1916), 28.

26. Journalist John L. O'Sullivan coined the phrase "manifest destiny" in 1839. He believed that unique and presumably inherent "American" (Anglo-Saxon) qualities of virtue and moral and civic greatness justified American dominance and accounted for its "unstoppable" nature. Available online at the PBS website, http://www.pbs.org/kera/usmexicanwar/resources/manifest_destiny_sullivan.html.

27. Dorothy Roberts, *Killing the Black Body: Race, Reproduction, and the Meaning of Liberty* (New York: Vintage Books, 1999), 23.

28. *Lothrop Stoddard: The Rising Tide of Color Against White World-Supremacy* (New York: Charles Scribner's Sons, 1921), 259–60.

29. Alan M. Kraut, *Silent Travelers: Germs, Genes, and the "Immigrant Menace"* (New York: Basic Books, 1994), 2.

30. Susan Sontag, *Illness as Metaphor* and *AIDS and Its Metaphors* (New York: Picador, 2001), 113.

31. Susan M. Schweik, *The Ugly Laws: Disability in Public* (New York: New York University Press, 2009), 165.

32. Paul A. Lombardo, *Three Generations, No Imbeciles: Eugenics, the Supreme Court and* Buck v. Bell (Baltimore: Johns Hopkins University Press, 2008), 293–94.

33. "Birth Control: The History of Sterilization Abuse in the United States," Our Bodies, Ourselves Health Resource Center, http://www

.ourbodiesourselves.org/book/companion.asp?id=18&compID=55, and "Case Docket: *Relf v. Weinberger*," Southern Poverty Law Center." See also Alexandra Minna Stern, "Sterilized in the Name of Public Health: Race, Immigration, and Reproductive Control in Modern California," *American Journal of Public Health* 95, no. 7 (2005): 1128–38; Jane Lawrence, "The Indian Health Service and the Sterilization of Native American Women, *American Indian Quarterly* 24, no. 3 (Summer 2000): 400–419; and Patrick McGreevy and Phil Wilson, "Female Inmate Surgery Broke Law," *Los Angeles Times,* July 14, 2013, http://articles.latimes.com/2013 /jul/14/local/la-me-prison-sterilization-20130714.

34. See "The Influence of the Private Prison Industry in Immigrant Detention," Detention Watch, http://www.detentionwatchnetwork.org /privateprisons.

35. Physicians for Human Rights, *Buried Alive: Solitary Confinement in the US Detention System,* 2013, http://physiciansforhumanrights.org/library/reports /buried-alive-solitary-confinement-in-the-us-detention-system.html.

36. For an excellent interactive summary of the abuse at Henry's Turkey Service in Iowa, and the events that ensued as it was more widely exposed, see Dan Berry, "The 'Boys' in the Bunkhouse," *New York Times,* March 9, 2014, http://www.nytimes.com/interactive/2014/03/09/us/the-boys-in-the -bunkhouse.html?_r=0.

37. Simone Weil, *The Iliad, Or the Poem of Force* (Wallingford, PA: Pendle Hill, 1957), 3.

38. Slavoj Zizek, *Violence* (New York: Picador, 2008), 9.

39. Iris Marion Young, *Justice and the Politics of Difference* (Princeton, NJ: Princeton University Press, 1990), 41.

40. Smith, *Conquest,* 3.

41. Ibid.

42. Jeffrey J. Pokorak, "Rape as a Badge of Slavery: The Legal History of, and Remedies for, Prosecutorial Race-of-Victim Charging Disparities," *Nevada Law Journal* 7, no. 1 (2006), article 2, http://scholars.law.unlv.edu /nlj/vol7/iss1/2.

43. Roni Caryn Rabin, "Nearly 1 in 5 Women in U.S. Survey Say They Have Been Sexually Assaulted," *New York Times,* December 14, 2011, http:// www.nytimes.com/2011/12/15/health/nearly-1-in-5-women-in-us-survey -report-sexual-assault.html?_r=0. See also Department of Defense Annual

Report on Sexual Assault in the Military Fiscal Year 2012 (Washington, DC: Department of Defense Sexual Assault Prevention and Response, 2013). See also Karen J. Terry et al., *The Causes and Context of Sexual Abuse of Minors by Catholic Priests in the United States, 1950–2010: A Report Presented to the United States Conference of Catholic Bishops by the John Jay College Research Team* (Washington, DC: United States Conference of Catholic Bishops, May 2011), http://www.bishop-accountability.org /reports/2011_05_18_John_Jay_Causes_and_Context_Report.pdf.

44. Just Detention International, http://www.justdetention.org/en/learn _the_basics.aspx.

CHAPTER 2: HATE IN THE PUBLIC IMAGINATION

Barry Lopez, from an interview in Poets and Writers 22, no. 2 (1994).

1. Susan Sontag, *On Photography* (New York: Farrar, Straus, and Giroux, 1977), 5.

2. Ibid., 19.

3. Pauline Kael, *Kiss Kiss Bang Bang* (Boston: Little, Brown, 1968), vii.

4. Anzia Yezierska, *Red Ribbons, White Horse* (New York: Persea, 1981), 40.

5. Edward W. Said, *Orientalism* (New York: Pantheon, 1978).

6. Sarah Lawrence and Jeremy Travis, *The New Landscape of Imprisonment: Mapping America's Prison Expansion* (Washington, DC: Urban Institute Justice Policy Center, 2004), http://www.urban.org/publications /410994.html. See also "Incarceration," Sentencing Project, http://www .sentencingproject.org/template/page.cfm?id=107.

CHAPTER 3: BOUNDARIES, BORDERS, AND PSYCHIC SHADOWS OF HATE

James Baldwin, Notes of a Native Son, in Baldwin: Collected Essays, ed. Toni Morrison (New York: The Library of America, 1998), 75.

1. *Powers of Horror: An Essay on Abjection*, trans. Leon S. Roudiez (New York: Columbia University Press, 1982), 65.

2. Simone Weil, *The Iliad or The Poem of Force* (Wallingford, PA: Pendle Hill, 1957), 3.

3. Simone Weil, *The Need for Roots: Prelude to a Declaration of Duties Towards Mankind* (New York: Harper, Colophon, 1972), 43.

4. See, for example, Kenneth O'Reilly, *"Racial Matters": The FBI's Secret File on Black America, 1960–1972* (New York: Free Press, 1991), 261–92. See also

Tim Weiner, *Enemies: A History of the FBI* (New York: Random House, 2013), 270–74.

5. US Department of Homeland Security, "Rightwing Extremism: Current Economic and Political Climate Refueling Resurgence in Radicalization and Recruitment," April 7, 2009. Available online at the Southern Poverty Law Center website, http://www.splcenter.org/get-informed/news/ homeland-security-economic-political-climate-fueling-extremism.

6. *New York Times*, November 3, 1997.

7. *New York Times*, January 29, 1998.

8. Season 8, episode 17.

9. The following states have laws that criminalize HIV transmission or potential transmission: Alabama, Alaska, Arkansas, California, Colorado, Delaware, Florida, Georgia, Idaho, Illinois, Indiana, Iowa, Kansas, Kentucky, Louisiana, Maryland, Michigan, Mississippi, Missouri, Montana, Nevada, New Jersey, New York, North Carolina, North Dakota, Ohio, Oklahoma, Pennsylvania, South Carolina, South Dakota, Tennessee, Texas, Utah, Virginia, and Washington. See http://data.lambdalegal.org/ publications/downloads/fs_hiv-criminalization.pdf.

10. Augustine of Hippo, *The City of God* (New York: Penguin Classics, 2003), 358.

11. "What Do We Mean By 'Evil'?" *New Yorker*, July 25, 2012 blog. Posted by Rollo Romig.

12. National Gay and Lesbian Task Force, *Injustice at Every Turn: A Report of the National Transgender Discrimination Survey* (February 2011), http:// www.thetaskforce.org/reports_and_research/ntds.

13. Michael Feldberg, *The Philadelphia Riots of 1844: A Study of Ethnic Conflict* (Westport, CT: Greenwood Press, 1975).

14. Peter Lewis Allen, *Wages of Sin: Sex and Disease, Past and Present* (Chicago: University of Chicago Press, 2000), 35.

15. William D. Mosher, Anjani Chandra, and Jo Jones, *Sexual Behavior and Selected Health Measures: Men and Women 15–44 Years of Age* (Washington, DC: U.S. Department of Health and Human Services, Division of Vital Statistics, September 15, 2005, http://www.avclub.com/article/ february-24–2010–38481.

16. Martha Nussbaum, *From Disgust to Humanity: Sexual Orientation and Constitutional Law* (New York: Oxford University Press, 2010), 2–5.

17. Simone Weil, *Gravity and Grace* (New York: Putnam, 1952), 123.

18. Nussbaum, *From Disgust*, 14–15.

19. Julia Layton, "How Fear Works," *HowStuffWorks*, http://science
.howstuffworks.com/life/fear.htm.

20. Herbert Marcuse, *Eros and Civilization: A Philosophical Inquiry into Freud*
(New York: Vintage, 1962), 13–17.

21. Nussbaum, *From Disgust*, 15.

22. Barry Glassner, *Fear: Why Americans Are Afraid of the Wrong Things* (New
York: Basic Books, 1999), 3.

23. Ibid., xxvi.

24. Slavoj Zizek, *Violence* (New York: Picador, 2008), 38.

25. Ibid., 41–46.

26. See, for example, Radley Balko, *Rise of the Warrior Cop: The Militarization
of America's Police Forces* (New York: Public Affairs, 2014).

27. The Sentencing Project, "Incarceration," http://www.sentencingproject
.org/template/page.cfm?id=107; "Women in the Justice System," http://
www.sentencingproject.org/template/page.cfm?id=138.

28. Quoted in John Dear, *Peace Behind Bars: A Peacemaking Priest's Journey
from Jail* (New York: Sheed and Ward, 1995), 65.

29. The Sentencing Project, "Racial Disparity," http://www.sentencingproject
.org/template/page.cfm?id=122.

30. Nancy A. Heitzeg, "Decriminalizing School Discipline," in *Enduring
Questions* (Praeger/ABC-CLIO, 2013), reprinted at *Critical Mass Progress*, February 12, 2014, http://criticalmassprogress.com/2014/02/12/ci
-decriminalizing-school-discipline/.

31. Chris Megerian, "California Prisons: Supreme Court Action a Setback
for Brown," *Los Angeles Times*, October 15, 2013, http://articles.latimes
.com/2013/oct/15/local/la-me-pc-california-jerry-brown-prisons-supreme
-court-20131015.

32. Saki Knafo and Chris Kirkham, "For-Profit Prisons Are Big Winners of
California's Overcrowding Crisis," *Huffington Post*, October 25, 2013, http://
www.huffingtonpost.com/2013/10/25/california-private-prison_n_4157641
.html.

33. Paige St. John, "California Prison Population Expected to Grow over
Next 5 Years," *Los Angeles Times*, January 9, 2014, http://www.latimes.com
/local/la-me-ff-prisons-20140110,0,1114998.story#axzz2q6hJWH2W.

CHAPTER 4: COLLECTIVE RESPONSIBILITY AND MORAL DISENGAGEMENT
Lillian Smith, "The Mob and the Ghost," *The Winner Names the Age: A Collection of Writings*, ed. Michelle Ciff (New York: W. W. Norton, 1982), 137–39.

1. Zizek, *Violence*, 43.

2. G. Flint Taylor and Joey L. Mogul, "'Sorry' Not Good Enough for Chicago Police Torture Survivors," *In These Times* (web only), January 6, 2014, http://inthesetimes.com/article/16064/sorry_not_good_enough_for _torture_surviors_say_activists/. See also the Chicago Police Torture page on the People's Law Office website, http://peopleslawoffice.com/issues -and-cases/chicago-police-torture/; and Andrea J. Ritchie and Joey L. Mogul, "In the Shadows of the War on Terror: Persistent Police Brutality and Abuse of People of Color in the United States," *DePaul Journal for Social Justice* 1, no. 2 (Spring 2008): 175.

3. See, for example, Craig B. Futterman, H. Melissa Mather, and Melanie Miles, "The Use of Statistical Evidence to Address Police Supervisory and Disciplinary Practices: The Chicago Police Department's Broken System," *DePaul Journal for Social Justice* 1, no. 2 (Spring 2008): 251. For examples of other reports documenting law enforcement violence throughout the United States, see Human Rights Watch, *Shielded from Justice: Police Brutality and Accountability in the United States* (1998), http://www.hrw .org/legacy/reports/reports98/police/download.htm. See also Amnesty International USA, *Stonewalled: Police Abuse and Misconduct Against Lesbian, Gay, Bisexual and Transgender People in the U.S.* (London: Amnesty International, 2005), http://www.amnesty.org/en/library/info/AMR51/122/2005.

4. Hannah Arendt, "Organized Guilt and Universal Responsibility," in *The Portable Hannah Arendt*, ed. Peter Baehr (New York: Penguin, 2000), 149–50.

5. Angela Y. Davis, "The Meaning of Freedom," in *The Meaning of Freedom and Other Difficult Dialogues* (San Francisco: City Lights, 2012), 79.

6. Arendt, "Organized Guilt," 154–55.

7. Eduardo Bonilla-Silva, *Racism Without Racists: Color-Blind Racism and the Persistence of Racial Inequality in America*, 3rd ed. (Lanham, MD: Rowman and Littlefield, 2009).

8. Everett C. Hughes, "Good People and Dirty Work," in *On Work, Race, and the Sociological Imagination*, ed. Louis A. Coser (Chicago: University of Chicago Press, 1994), 184.

9. Kathleen M. Blee, *Women of the Klan: Racism and Gender in the 1920s*, with a new preface (1991; repr., Berkeley: University of California Press, 2009), viii, 1–3. See also Kathleen Blee, "Becoming a Racist: Women in Contemporary Ku Klux Klan and Neo-Nazi Groups," *Gender and Society* 10, no. 6 (1996): 694.

10. Robert Jay Lifton, *The Nazi Doctors: Medical Killing and the Psychology of Genocide* (1986; repr., New York: Basic Books, 2000), 4–5.

11. Wendy Lower, *Hitler's Furies: German Women in the Nazi Killing Fields* (New York: Houghton Mifflin Harcourt, 2013).

12. Philip Gourevitch, *We Wish to Inform You That Tomorrow We Will Be Killed With Our Families: Stories from Rwanda* (New York: Picador, 1999), 137–38.

13. Hughes, "Good People and Dirty Work," 186–87.

14. See, for example, Rita Nakashima Brock and Gabriella Lettini, *Soul Repair: Recovering from Moral Injury after War* (Boston: Beacon Press, 2013). See also Robert Jay Lifton, *Home from the War: Learning from Vietnam Veterans* (1973; repr., New York: Other Press, 2005).

15. Gary Lindberg, *The Confidence Man in American Literature* (New York: Oxford University Press, 1982), 3–12.

16. Margaret Mead and James Baldwin, *A Rap on Race* (Philadelphia: J. P. Lippincott, 1971), 59.

17. "Economic Justice for All: Pastoral Letter on Catholic Social Teaching and the U.S. Economy," US Conference of Catholic Bishops, November 1, 1986, online at the Berkeley Center for Religion, Peace, and World Affairs, http://berkleycenter.georgetown.edu/resources/publications/economic -justice-for-all-pastoral-letter-on-catholic-social-teaching-and-the-u-s -economy.

18. Milton Friedman, "Good Ends, Bad Means," in *The Catholic Challenge to the American Economy: Reflections on the U.S. Bishops' Pastoral Letter on Catholic Social Teaching and the U.S. Economy* (New York: Macmillan, 1987), 99, 105.

19. Peter Kornbluh, "CIA Acknowledges Ties to Pinochet's Repression," National Security Archive, Chile Documentation Project, September 19, 2000, http://www2.gwu.edu/fflnsarchiv/news/20000919/. This summary of findings includes links to documents released publicly by the CIA.

20. William T. Cavanaugh, *Torture and Eucharist* (Malden, MA: Blackwell, 1998), 28, 39, 47, 278–79.

21. The Center for Justice and Accountability, *Chile: The Pinochet Years*, http://www.cja.org/article.php?list=type&type=196.

22. See, for example, J. Patrice McSherry, *Predatory States: Operation Condor and Covert War in Latin America* (Lanham, MD: Rowman & Littlefield, 2005).

23. Arendt, "Organized Guilt," 154.

24. See, for example, Larry May and Stacey Hoffman, eds., *Collective Responsibility: Five Decades of Debate in Theoretical and Applied Ethics* (Lanham, MD: Rowman & Littlefield, 1991).

25. Susan Sontag, "The Conscience of Words," in *At the Same Time: Essays & Speeches* (New York: Picador, 2007), 152.

26. Robert Jay Lifton, *Hiroshima in America: A Half Century of Denial* (New York: Avon Books, 1996), xiv.

27. Angela Y. Davis, "Report from Harlem," in *The Meaning of Freedom*, 30–31.

28. Patricia Hill Collins, *Black Feminist Thought: Knowledge, Consciousness, and the Politics of Empowerment* (Boston: Unwin Hyman, 1990), 221–22.

29. See, for example, the documentary film *Hey, Boo: Harper Lee and To Kill a Mockingbird*, written, produced, and directed by Mary McDonagh Murphy (Mary Murphy & Company, 2010).

30. Austin Sarat and Martha Merrill Umphrey, eds., *Reimagining* To Kill a Mockingbird: *Family, Community, and the Possibility of Equal Justice Under Law* (Amherst: University of Massachusetts Press, 2013).

31. Morrison, *Playing in the Dark*, 51–53.

32. Thomas Mallon, "Big Bird: A Biography of the Novelist Harper Lee," review of *Mockingbird: A Portrait of Harper Lee*, by Charles J. Shield, *New Yorker*, May 29, 2006, http://www.newyorker.com/archive/2006/05/29/060529crbo_books?currentPage=all.

33. Lynching was never just a Southern phenomenon, and though the overwhelming majority of people killed were black, this extralegal violence also took the lives of American Indians, Mexicans, Asians, other unwanted immigrants, and purported lawbreakers, some of whom were white and said to be beyond the reach of formal systems of law enforcement. See James Allen, Hilton Als, Congressman John Lewis, and Leon F. Litwack, *Without Sanctuary: Lynching Photography in America* (Santa Fe, NM: Twin Palms, 2000). See also Amy Louise

Wood, *Lynching and Spectacle: Witnessing Racial Violence in America, 1890–1940* (Chapel Hill: University of North Carolina Press, 2009); Ken Gonzales-Day, *Lynching in the West 1850–1935* (Durham, NC: Duke University Press, 2006); and Sherrilyn A. Ifill, *On the Courthouse Lawn: Confronting the Legacy of Lynching in the Twenty-First Century* (Boston: Beacon Press, 2007).

34. Ida B. Wells-Barnett, *The Red Record: Tabulated Statistics and Alleged Causes of Lynching in the United States* (1895). See also Jacqueline Jones Royster, ed., *Southern Horrors and Other Writings: The Anti-Lynching Campaign of Ida B. Wells, 1892–1900* (Boston: Bedford/St. Martin's, 1997).

35. Allen et al., *Without Sanctuary.*

36. James H. Cone, *The Cross and the Lynching Tree* (Maryknoll, NY: Orbis Press, 2012), xiii.

37. Smith, "The Mob and the Ghost," 137–39.

38. Zizek, *Violence*, 41–45.

39. Rev. Martin Luther King Jr., "A Knock at Midnight," in *A Knock at Midnight: Inspiration from the Great Sermons of Reverend Martin Luther King, Jr.*, ed. Clayborne Carson and Peter Holloran (New York: Warner Books, 1998), 61–78.

CHAPTER 5: GOODNESS IN THE PUBLIC IMAGINATION

Quoted in Sarah Schulman, The Gentrification of the Mind: Witness to a Lost Generation (Berkeley: University of California Press, 2012), 52

1. "The National Security Strategy of the United States of America," Office of the President of the United States, September 2002, http://www.state .gov/documents/organization/63562.pdf.

2. Lawrence Thornton, *Imagining Argentina* (New York: Bantam Books, 1988), 65. In *Torture and Eucharist*, William T. Cavanaugh discusses the importance of Thornton's novel to understanding a similar contest of imaginations in Chile during the Pinochet dictatorship.

3. Luise Puenzo's 1985 feature film *The Official Story* tells the fictional story of a mother who is raising one of these children as she begins to question the circumstances of her adopted daughter's arrival.

4. For a detailed account, see Marguerite Guzman Bouvard, *Revolutionizing Motherhood: The Mothers of the Plaza de Mayo* (Lanham, MD: Rowman & Littlefield, 2002).

5. See, for example, Greg Myre, "The Day Nelson Mandela Walked Out of Prison," National Public Radio, June 27, 2013, http://www.npr.org/blogs/parallels/2013/06/11/190671704/the,-day-nelson-mandela-walked-out-of-prison.

6. Final reports of the South African Truth and Reconciliation Commission are online at http://www.justice.gov.za/Trc/report/index.htm.

7. Transitional justice, according to the International Center for Transitional Justice, "refers to the set of judicial and non-judicial measures that have been implemented by different countries in order to redress the legacies of massive human rights abuses." Elements of transitional justice (specific processes vary according to the needs of particular communities or nations) may include criminal prosecutions, reparations, institutional reform, truth commissions (or other means to investigate, report on, and redress systematic patterns of abuse), and more. For more information, see ICTJ website: http://ictj.org.

8. There are many different critical perspectives on the processes, significance, and outcomes of the South African Truth and Reconciliation Commission. For one useful discussion that gathers a variety of perspectives, see Jacobus A. Du Pisani and Kwang-Su Kim, "Establishing the Truth about the Apartheid Past: Historians and the South African Truth and Reconciliation Commission," *African Studies Quarterly* 8, no. 1 (Fall 2004): 78–95, http://www.africa.ufl.edu/ASQ/v8/v8i1a5.htm.

9. Paul Tullis, "Can Forgiveness Play a Role in Criminal Justice?" *New York Times*, January 4, 2013, http://www.nytimes.com/2013/01/06/magazine/can-forgiveness-play-a-role-in-criminal-justice.html?pagewanted=all.

10. For useful discussions of the promises and limitations of restorative justice, see Zeher Institute for Restorative Justice, Eastern Mennonite University, "Restorative Justice? What's That?," http://www.emu.edu/cjp/restorative-justice/what-is-rj/. See also Katherine Whitlock, *In a Time of Broken Bones: A Call to Dialogue on Hate Violence and the Limitations of Hate Crimes Legislation* (Philadelphia: American Friends Service Committee, 2001), 21–25, https://afsc.org/document/time-broken-bones.

11. For links to useful resources on various Indigenous approaches to justice, see Living Justice Press, "Indigenous Approaches to Justice," http://www.livingjusticepress.org/.

12. Cornelius Castoriadis, *The Imaginary Institution of Society*, trans. Kathleen Blamey (Cambridge, MA: MIT Press, 1998), 149. This work originally appeared in French under the title *L'institution imaginaire de la société* (Paris: Editions du Seuil, 1975).

13. Scot Nakagawa, "Blackness Is the Fulcrum," *Race Files*, May 4, 2012, http://www.racefiles.com/2012/05/04/blackness-is-the-fulcrum/

14. Lewis Hyde, *The Gift: Creativity and the Artist in the Modern World*, 2nd ed. (New York: Vintage Books), xii.

15. See, for example, Dorothy E. Roberts, "Prison, Foster Care, and the Systemic Punishment of Black Mothers," *UCLA Law Review* 59 (2012): 1474–1500.

16. Sarah Schulman, *The Gentrification of the Mind: Witness to a Lost Imagination* (Berkeley: University of California Press, 2012), 14, 47.

17. Lewis Hyde, *Trickster Makes This World: Mischief, Myth, and Art* (1988; repr., New York: Farrar, Straus and Giroux, 2010), 9, 13.

18. James Baldwin, "The Artist's Struggle for Integrity," in *James Baldwin and the Cross of Redemption: Uncollected Writings*, ed. Randall Kenan (New York: Vintage Books, 2010), 51.

19. Christina B. Hanhardt, *Safe Space: Gay Neighborhood History and the Politics of Violence* (Durham, NC: Duke University Press, 2013), 30.

20. Robert Coles, *The Call to Stories: Teaching and the Moral Imagination* (Boston: Houghton Mifflin, 1990), 196.

21. Robert Jay Lifton, "Conversations with History," October 2001. Institute of International Studies at the University of California, Berkeley, series host Harry Kreisler. Video at http://conversations.berkeley.edu/content/robert-jay-lifton; transcript at http://globetrotter.berkeley.edu/people/Lifton/lifton-cono.html.

22. Thomas Norman DeWolf and Sharon Leslie Morgan, *Gather at the Table: The Healing Journey of a Daughter of Slavery and a Son of the Slave Trade* (Boston: Beacon Press, 2012).

23. Howard Thurman, *The Search for Common Ground: An Inquiry into the Basis of Man's Experience of Community* (1971; repr., Richmond, IN: Friends United Press, 1986), 67.

24. Barry Lopez, "Eden Is a Conversation," 2006, Barry Lopez website, http://www.barrylopez.com/_eden_is_a_conversation__59075.htm.

25. Ari Berman, "North Carolina's Moral Monday Movement Kicks Off 2014 With a Massive Rally in Raleigh," *Nation*, February 8, 2014.

26. Audre Lorde, "The Transformation of Silence into Language and Action," in *Sister Outsider: Essays & Speeches* (Freedom, CA: Crossing Press, 1984), 42. This was from a speech Lorde gave in 1977.

27. Mishuana Goeman, *Mark My Words: Native Women Mapping Our Nations* (Minneapolis: University of Minnesota Press, 2013), 2, 3.

28. Toni Morrison, "Goodness: Altruism and the Literary Imagination." 2012 Harvard Divinity School Ingersoll Lecture on Immortality, December 6, 2012. Online at http://www.hds.harvard.edu/multimedia/video/goodness -altruism-and-the-literary-imagination. Summary: http://news.harvard .edu/gazette/story/2012/12/good-but-never-simple/.

INDEX